BIENVENIDA

BIENVENIDA

THE MAKING OF
A MODERN MISTRESS

COUNTESS BIENVENIDA SOKOLOW

SMITH GRYPHON
PUBLISHERS

First published in Great Britain in 1996 by
SMITH GRYPHON LIMITED
12 Bridge Wharf, 156 Caledonian Road
London N1 9UU

A CIP catalogue record for this book is available from the British Library

ISBN 1 85685 112 5

Typeset by Creative Print and Design Group, Harmondsworth
Printed in Great Britain by Butler & Tanner Ltd, Frome

CONTENTS

Acknowledgements   vi

1. Simple Beginnings   1

2. Ignorance and Cruelty   11

3. A Glimpse of the Possible   27

4. The Learning Process   45

5. Application   71

6. Toys and Texas   97

7. Becoming Lady Buck   119

8. Trapped in a Nightmare   129

9. The Centre of Power   143

10. The Depths of Despair   153

11. Supping with the Devil   169

12. Emerging from the Wreckage   179

ACKNOWLEDGEMENTS

I would like to thank Andrew Crofts for his assistance in the preparation of this book. And my literary agent, Jeffrey Simmons, for his kind support and patience, Diana Colbert, my publicity agent, for her professionalism, and my publisher, Robert Smith, for making it all possible.

1

Simple Beginnings

*I*t is, of course, impossible to know whether or not my life would have taken the same course if I had been born into a happier and more balanced family. However, my comparatively humble origins, for which I make absolutely no apologies or excuses, were certainly a strong motivating force, as were a number of incidents which I witnessed and experienced at a formative age.

I was born Maria-Bienvenida Pérez Blanco in the Spanish city of Valencia, on 15 February 1957. Valencia itself is situated on the east coast in the centre of a wide, fertile plain called the Huerta and in 1962 the city achieved two thousand years of existence. Originally a Roman port on the Iberian Peninsula, it was in fact one of the first Roman strongholds, immortalized in the film *El Cid* starring Charlton Heston and Sophia Loren. In the thirteenth century it fell under Muslim domination for nearly one hundred and fifty years. Valencia is a city that has, in essence, changed very little in the past few centuries, yet there has been a remarkable emergence of talented and artistic young people within the past five decades.

My earliest memories are of being a happy little girl knowing nothing of the outside world and quite content in the environment in which I lived. I remember little of my mother, who left me in the care of my maternal grandmother, Francisca, at the age of two, when she went to London to find work. My grandmother, although physically fragile, was nonetheless a powerful, matriarchal figure. She had had four children of her own, to whom she had strong allegiance, and did not suffer fools gladly. Her husband Pedro having died many years earlier, she had been obliged to take control of her whole family and she ran her household and finances with a rod of iron.

I have perhaps painted a rather bleak picture of my grandmother, for she was, in fact, a warm and loving woman, though of limited intellect and emotional vision, who looked after not only me but my cousin Rosita, who was a few months older than me. Rosita, whose mother had died in childbirth, had also been left with my grandmother while her father, Manuel, had gone off to live and work in France with his new wife, Carmen. However, rather than considering Rosita as a sister, I regarded her as a rival for my grandmother's affections and there developed between us a strong sense of competition. It did not stop us playing together and sharing our childhood, but I always felt, I believe with some justification, that I was the less popular of the two.

The house in which I was born belonged to my father and for a brief two years we all lived there before my mother left for London. I have never fully resolved the question of why my parents ever got married. She certainly never loved him and they were never happy together or even remotely suited in any way. For two years after my mother's departure my father, Francisco, a kind, gentle man of deep religious convictions, lived with us. He had a workshop on the ground floor of the house, and here he mended clocks and watches, as well as household goods such as cutlery and electrical items. As far as I was concerned, his workshop was a treasure cave full of mysterious and exciting objects and I remember on one occasion playing a game with a machine that polished cutlery. Being nimble, I had taken to using the leather belt attached to the machine's motor as an improvised skipping rope. With hindsight I can definitely say that a workshop is far from an ideal location in which a child should be playing, for the inevitable happened. The little short dress I was wearing got caught in the machine, which promptly jammed. I was badly frightened by the incident and everyone was terribly cross with me, but it did not stop me from playing in the workshop – only I was a little more careful the next time, having learnt from my experience.

The three-floor house in which we lived was in a district of Valencia known as El Carmen, the oldest part of the city, which was built up firstly by the Romans and then, in the thirteenth century, by the Moors from North Africa. The house was built on the corner of the Calle Alta, a street which divided the nobility and their grand mansions from the market area and the dwellings of the humbler classes. The entire area, now cared for by the Patrimonio Nacional (National Heritage), comprises the Museo de Bellas Artes, La Catedral de Valencia, El Ayuntamiento, La Iglesia de Los Santos Juanes and La Lonja, among other treasures. The house, with my father's small workshop on the ground floor, was comfortable but Spartan, and perhaps it was this absence of luxury that drove my mother to seek work and a better standard of living in London.

She had had a perfectly good job in Valencia as a maid to the man whom she had asked to be my godfather, Rafael Vásquez, a prominent paediatrician, but felt that there were greater and better opportunities awaiting her in London, to which Spanish people have always been attracted, for it represents to them a wondrous city paved with gold. I had no such aspirations in my childhood and, despite the paucity of comforts, I was quite content living in the little backstreet house, simply because I knew no different. My earliest recollections of my mother are that she was beautiful and elegant, despite her humble employment, and in the little I saw of her in my formative years she was both kind and generous.

In October 1957, when I was only nine months old, Valencia was struck by some of the most dreadful floods in the city's history. They lasted for two or even three months and the damage was far more serious and extensive than in any previous floods. Nature is not selective in its destructive forces and it was not only the smaller houses that suffered but the beautiful old mansions as well. The catastrophe obliged the civic authorities, and ultimately the national government, to fund the diversion of the River Turia, which then ran through the middle of Valencia, so that the river would then irrigate the agricultural areas to the south of the city and never again pose a threat to its beautiful buildings. This huge engineering project was known as the Plan Sur, and by 1961, when the undertaking was completed, the old river bed had been transformed by the famous Catalan architect Ricardo Bofil, into public gardens and the Palacio de la Música.

With my father's workshop, and therefore his home, lost as a result of the floods, the family's financial situation suffered considerably, as did the fortunes of many Valencians at the time. My mother, who considered my father a weak and ineffective man with little or no ambition, was ultimately to use the loss of the workshop and income as an excuse to seek work in London. After the flood, it was my grandmother's ability to adapt to an even more frugal lifestyle that was to see us through a very hard time. Over a period of eighteen months my father rebuilt his little workshop and life more or less resumed its natural course.

In terms of my development as a child I was no different from any other of the neighbourhood children except perhaps that, because I had very long, dark-blonde hair, pale skin and green eyes, I was somewhat more conspicuous. I had, however, very mixed feelings about my mother and consequently about what an ideal family life should be. On the one hand I was proud and excited that she was in London, which to me was an exotic and wonderful, almost magical place. On the other hand I was very conscious of her absence and my need to be nurtured, loved and cared for. I do not feel that my grandmother catered for these needs, not because of an unwillingness on her part but as a result of an unconscious preference for my cousin Rosita. After all, she was a frail child, her mother had died giving birth to her and Manuel, her father, was my grandmother's eldest son. I, by contrast, was the result of an incidental and perhaps unfortunate union between my mother and a man whom, though I loved him, everyone regarded as a weak-willed and rather ineffectual individual. Thus, my cousin was regarded with a strong degree of sympathy, whereas I was sometimes treated with barely disguised contempt.

I was a playful child and enjoyed being with other children of my own age, even boys, with whom I cavorted in the street. We played games in and around the doorsteps of the neighbourhood, where the old men and women sat clad in their perpetual black clothes, passing silent judgement on the moulds in which their colourless lives had been cast. I was as carefree and innocent as all the other children. I do remember being particularly adroit at all the street games, such as hide-and-seek, marbles, skipping and the game called hopscotch in English, where we marked out the pavement with chalk and had to jump from one numbered paving stone to another. Throughout my time in Valencia one of the main sources of entertainment was listening to the radio, and I loved to dance to the music emanating from within the large brown wireless. I remember going into the small, crowded local shops to dance and sing for the amusement of the shopkeepers, their customers and anyone else who would watch.

Back in the late fifties and sixties there was little danger within the city communities in which we lived. Everyone was aware of everyone else's business within the boundaries of a few streets and the proud Spanish tradition of loyalty ensured that, despite differences within a family, a dedication to the presentation of unity was paramount. I was a particular favourite with the old women of the neighbourhood, who would either sit on their hard chairs on their doorsteps or busy themselves with endless domestic chores in their darkened houses. To me they would call an affectionate greeting as I passed and would come out to admire my long hair and pale skin. Frequently they would give me sweets or other little gifts while ruffling my hair with their calloused hands, touched by my high spirits. I, of course, enjoyed the attention, as would any child who, lacking affection at home, inevitably seeks the approval and warmth of others.

When I was about five, the family managed to scrape enough money together to buy a sixth-floor flat in the Calle Literato Azorín, in an area of Valencia known as Ruzafa, not far from my father's house. My mother, despite her absence in England and my not having seen her since the age of two, had persuaded her sister, Francisca, and brother, Antonio, to help her buy the apartment, and she had contributed with the money she was earning in England. Part of the reason for the move was that my mother wanted to remove me from my father's influence altogether, as well as the fact that it irked her that her mother and daughter were living under his roof.

I remember that the flat was airy and sunny and very different from my father's simple home. Here I was to remain for some eighteen months to two years and my father, although not divorced from my mother then or ever, was granted visiting rights one Sunday a month. He would arrive smartly dressed in a suit and tie, bringing me small gifts and tokens of his affection. I loved him dearly and I don't doubt that he also loved me in return or else he would not have taken the time and trouble to visit me. As a devoutly religious man he would take me to church, where he would hold my hand as we sat in silence, both of us overwhelmed by the solemnity and dignity of the proceedings.

My father had been left behind in his little house, where, without my giving the matter any thought, doubtless he continued to earn a meagre living operating the simple machinery in his workshop during the day and sitting in solitude listening to the radio in the evenings. There may or may not have been any discussion about the move from his house to the flat, but either way my father would not have put up much of a fight. Already emotionally vanquished by my mother, against whom he never found the strength to stand up, his attitude was one of *Deo Volente* and resignation to whatever situations life chose to throw at him. No doubt he found some solace in his religious convictions. To this day I don't know what lay behind my mother's attitude towards him. Perhaps it was that he served as a constant reminder of a moment of weakness in her life. As a small child I never questioned the behaviour of adults. I simply accepted that one's parents and family act correctly according to a set of rules which children are too young to comprehend but accept unquestioningly at all times. It is only later in life that we learn to question the actions of our elders, having previously placed them on a pedestal upon which they remain unassailable until adolescence and early adulthood enlighten us about their human weaknesses and fallibility.

My grandmother, despite her advancing years, was, in the absence of my mother, still the rock upon which my life was built. She had obviously sided with my mother over the move from my father's house, for financial reasons as well as out of family loyalty. Having moved, however, my mother virtually forbade all contact with my father, except for the monthly visits, and I never again met any of his family despite the fact that a number of them, in particular my aunt Segundina and her husband Emilio were, like my father, kind, tender and warm people. I don't remember missing my father, although I must have done. In addition I must have found it most odd that the so-called family life which I left behind each morning to go to school and returned to each afternoon, centred around my cousin Rosita, a weak and sickly child, and my grandmother, who continued to be a tower of strength. As long as she was there with her strong arms, stern words and rigorous regime, I felt that no harm would come to me and I could allow my mother to continue to be the glamorous fantasy figure of whom I was so proud and whom I had mistakenly elevated to such an unwarranted status.

Manuel, Rosita's father and my grandmother's eldest son, was a construction worker by profession. He had moved to France in search of work soon after the death of his first wife, having remarried a harmless and gentle woman called Carmen. He had rented a farmhouse in the countryside near Montelimar, a large town situated on the River Rhône in the southeast of the country and best known for its fine-quality nougat. In 1963, when I was six, it was decided that Rosita, my grandmother and I should all move from the apartment in Valencia to Manuel's farmhouse. My grandmother wanted to be with her son and as she grew older she was finding it increasingly difficult to look after two small girls who were constantly making more and more demands on her energy and patience.

For about two years I was very happy living at the farmhouse. During the day I cycled to school, where I soon picked up the language and in the late afternoons and evenings I was quite content to sit and read any number of fairy stories, as they kept me entranced for hours. Of course I had my school friends and Rosita, with whom I still played. She was ecstatic to be reunited with her father and, although happy for her, I was inevitably jealous that she at least had one parent to love and cherish her. I very much enjoyed the freedom of the farm and although my uncle and his wife kept only chickens and rented just the farmhouse and yard, but no land, it was an exciting environment for me and I spent hours wandering through the vineyards and feeding the chickens as well as collecting their eggs.

Sadly, my grandmother's fortitude and health began to fail her and increasingly the burden of looking after Rosita and me fell on the shoulders of Carmen, Manuel's second wife. I remember her reading my favourite fairy tales to me, but I also remember how she used to suffer at the hands of my uncle, a brute of a man who, when drunk, which he frequently was, used to beat her up viciously and without remorse in front of us all. His beatings were ferocious and appalling to witness, but I remember that my grandmother, who was relying on his continuing financial support and hospitality, never uttered a word of reproach. For a little girl of six to witness such unprovoked violence was traumatic and something I have never forgotten. To this day I abhor violence of any kind and the drunken behaviour of men fills me with an unimaginable degree of disgust and loathing. Years later I myself was to suffer the consequences of a drunken and violent relationship which, although the harm was more emotional than physical, was, nonetheless just as painful and grisly.

By the age of seven I was becoming acutely aware of my mother's absence but my fears of abandonment were usually appeased by my grandmother, who would explain that her daughter had gone to England in order to support me, which she did by sending money whenever she could to help us get by. I recall the one occasion when my mother did come and visit us at the farm. I was totally overwhelmed by this beautiful and, to me, exotic-looking woman who had flown in on an aeroplane with neatly packed suitcases which, as far as I was concerned, contained all the mysteries and secrets of the world. My mother's visit was fairly fleeting but I remember her as being attentive, loving and apparently concerned about my well-being. Then again, one visit to her only daughter in four years cannot be deemed an enormous sacrifice and, of course, spending only a couple of weeks with me in no way made up for her long absence. In my eyes, however, she retained her lofty position on a pedestal, for she was not only my mother but also an exciting, romantic and wondrous woman not far removed from the fairy stories in which I lost myself every night.

By March of 1965 it was decided that we should return to the flat in Valencia, leaving behind my uncle Manuel and his wife. As we had done on the way to France, the three of us took the train back to Spain and soon resumed our old lives in Calle Literato Azorín, although by now my grandmother's health was failing badly. I was eight years old and went back to seeing my father one Sunday a month, as he still contributed to my upkeep. I was enjoying my schooling more and more, hungry for knowledge and desperately curious for any information that would give me a better idea of life outside the confines of our narrow little streets. In particular I enjoyed geography and history and wanted to learn all I could about the world which had lured away my mother. I was acutely aware that everything I wanted to know could be found in the pages of books and in the heads of my teachers and I searched doggedly, asking endless questions.

There was a very famous teenage actress and singer in the early sixties in Spain called Marisol. She was the idol of most little Spanish girls and I was no exception in wanting to model myself on her. It is quite normal and healthy for a child to want to shine and be like a star, and I longed to stand up and perform for adoring people, all of whom would love me for being beautiful, talented and successful. Of course, I continued to seek the approval of all around me but most of all I sought the approval of my mother, still far away in London. I recall thinking that if I were to become another Marisol, then my mother would be proud of me, would want to have me with her and I would have earned her love. In this era the film industry in Spain was strong and my frequent visits to the local open-air cinema, where my grandmother and I used to eat our picnic dinner, simply fuelled a dormant urge in me to become someone other than the barely tolerated and virtually abandoned little girl that I was in reality. I cannot deny that I was deeply influenced by the excursions to that and the other small, cramped and overheated cinemas we used to attend with such religious devotion.

My mother still made fleeting and infrequent visits to Valencia and each time I couldn't wait to see her. I was desperate for her to either visit or for her to send for me to join her in England. I remember receiving postcards from London that filled me with wonder and amazement as only a child can be fascinated and mesmerized by such small tokens. The buildings were huge, the streets modern and crowded with smart-looking people, the soldiers resplendent in their scarlet tunics and on their black horses. I urgently wanted to be with her, to share in the excitement and novelty. To me she was the luckiest person in the world and the old black-and-white photograph of her, elegant, upright and glamorous-looking, served only to elevate her aura further. I fancied that she looked not unlike the great Ava Gardner and was a far cry from the neighbourhood women, constantly working at their chores, aged and sexless before their time, with hands as big as those of their menfolk. My mother, her face unblemished by the ravages of time and unrewarded hard work, was totally unlike those old women, with their faces cracked and deeply lined, their bodies shapeless and bulky and always shrouded in black.

I would ask my grandmother, 'Why can't I go to England with her?' and she would reply, 'Because of the immigration laws,' without looking up from whatever chore occupied her at the time. She would answer me patiently until eventually I asked the same question so many times that she lost her temper. 'Because she is not your mother at all,' she snapped once. 'She just found you in the street and picked you up!' She then turned her back on me to signify that she no longer wished to continue the discussion, confident that she had finally found an answer to my pestering questions that would silence me once and for all. Her harsh words were like a searing knife in my heart, bringing tears to my eyes and the blood to my cheeks. Of course, I discovered that what she had said wasn't true but it left an indelible picture of my mother in my mind. From then on, my every feeling of insecurity was made worse by the growing belief that my birth had been a terrible mistake and that I was a burden on my family. I do not believe that my grandmother ever had any idea just how wounding her careless words were. She was much too busy with keeping the household going and looking after other people to worry about the feelings of a sensitive nine-year-old girl.

My mother had a younger sister called Francisca, a stunning-looking woman whom she eventually invited to England once she was settled. When Francisca came back to visit her family in Valencia she would talk to my grandmother about life with my mother in London as if I were not in the room, or maybe they thought that I was too young to understand what they were saying. I would sit quietly at the back of the kitchen or on the bus and listen intently to their incessant chatter even though I didn't understand a good deal of what they were discussing. I recall my aunt complaining about how difficult and unkind my mother was. Phrases such as 'she is so selfish' and 'Maria [my mother] has no heart' seem to have stuck in my mind, the second of these being particularly prophetic.

Curiously, my father never said a bad word against my mother or anyone for that matter. It was not in his nature to speak badly of others and I truly believe that all his kindness, patience and virtue were from the heart, whereas my mother seemed to put on these attributes for the sake of convenience. My memory of him in those early years is of a quiet, humble and diligent man in his workshop, calm and long-suffering, making no demands on the few people around him and expecting little from them in return. When my grandmother wasn't around, Aunt Francisca, whom I loved very much, would patiently indulge my childish fantasies and would allow me to play with her make-up, painting my adolescent lips and rouging my pale cheeks.

2

Ignorance and Cruelty

My grandmother, that stalwart pillar on whom so much of my emotional security depended, passed away when I was ten years old. The effect on my entire well-being was devastating for a number of reasons.

I had been told that my cousin Rosita had finally been sent to a special clinic in Barcelona that would cater for her distressingly debilitating mental condition, most probably brought about by abuse as a small infant. Also, I was told that she had gone to join her father and stepmother in France. This meant that I was now more or less the centre of my grandmother's world and not competing for attention with poor Rosita. In the event, the time for which only my grandmother and I were together in the apartment was fairly short-lived, but I remember being quite happy in that period.

The serious deterioration in my grandmother's health was sudden and the time between her relapse and her death was comparatively short. Before she was taken into hospital she remained in her bed at home on an intravenous drip suspended over her like some indifferent and transparent plastic witness to her imminent demise. As the only other person in the flat I was obliged to sleep next to her in the bed in order to ensure that either she didn't need anything in the night or there wasn't some crisis which I probably would not have been emotionally equipped to deal with anyway.

I was absolutely terrified that my grandmother would die while I was lying beside her, leaving me on my own in the apartment with no one else to watch over me. I remember deliberately willing myself to stay awake, listening intently to her laboured breathing until I was finally overcome by sheer exhaustion, when I would fall into a fitful sleep, punctuated by nightmares and confusing images.

Over a period of days the wasting disease from which she was suffering gradually sapped what little strength she had left and I recall her saying to me, 'If I die, you know where everything is in the kitchen. You know what to do. You will have to take care of all the arrangements for me.' I would nod solemnly and fight back the tears at the probable prospect of losing the only person who had stuck by me through my childhood. I didn't want to be left on my own to make the funeral arrangements – I had no idea where to start – and the concept of being left alone seemed too frightening to even contemplate. I had been constantly reminded of how hard my mother was working for my benefit in London and was not sure that she would appear in time to relieve me of the burden of my dying grandmother before the old lady passed away. Despite my efforts to block out the thought of finally losing her, the terrible ache of uncertainty and unhappiness prevailed and I tried desperately to prolong her life through sheer will-power. I wanted to force time to stand still so that I would not have to face the grief and emptiness which would inevitably follow her death. But the minutes and hours continued their silent chant as I sat and lay next to my grandmother as she grew weaker with each passing moment until even talking to me became too much of an effort for her.

At the last moment, just as the old woman's strength reached its lowest ebb, my mother arrived in Valencia from London. She wanted to be with her mother when she died and I was finally released from my fear of being left alone in the flat with the body of my grandmother growing cold in the room next to mine. My concerns about my future prevailed, however, although I distinctly remember thinking that with my grandmother in heaven as I had been told she would be, and no other members of the family in a position to look after me, my mother would finally be obliged to take me with her to London.

Shortly before my grandmother was moved into the local hospital, my father, always the gentleman, came to pay his final respects to the old lady who had so diligently looked after his only child. My mother was present when my father arrived and she shouted at him, 'How dare you come to my home! Get out!' Without saying so much as a word, he departed with great dignity, either unwilling or unable to stand up to her seemingly unprovoked anger. My mother's reaction was undignified, completely unwarranted and upset me most terribly. I could not understand what must have happened between my parents to cause such an outburst. Realizing that I was in distress, my mother tried to placate me, saying that she didn't want him there and how much he had hurt her in the past. 'He doesn't love you and he is not like a normal man should be,' she added. Of course I had no idea what she was talking about, but I can only suppose that from her point of view it was the ultimate insult one could pay a man.

I was still at a time in my life when I believed that adults always had the best interests of their offspring at heart and was willing to accept that in some unknown way my father had done something terrible and unforgivable to my mother. Until then and for a considerable time afterwards nobody had ever told me the truth. Perhaps their intentions were good – I don't know – but their well-meaning words kept me completely ignorant about much that was going on around me. Throughout my childhood I had listened uncomprehendingly to the neighbourhood women gossiping and arguing about everything. Everyone had an apparently valid opinion on all aspects of everyone else's life. Little of their chatter made any sense and as a result I was never certain of the truth about anything within the narrow confines of my own existence. In the absence of certainty, and constantly in receipt of conflicting facts, I had formed my own opinions about life, my family and relationships. These views were to be endorsed by further turbulent events in my life.

Although I had no idea then, it was the last time I would see my father for sixteen years. I was too concerned about my own future and welfare to reflect at length on my parents' estrangement. I was still at a vulnerable age where I constantly felt bewildered and lonely, and all I wanted was for my mother to sweep me up in her arms and take me away from all the misery, pain and sorrow heralded by the death of my grandmother.

The old lady died a few days after being admitted to hospital and for some reason probably based on a mixture of morbid tradition and sheer insensitivity, my mother took me down to the hospital morgue to see my grandmother laid out in her coffin. There were other bodies also awaiting visitors and I was terrified by the experience. 'You must kiss her,' my mother told me, so, shaking with fear, I bent down to kiss the peaceful-looking face. The old lady's cheek felt cold to my lips and her face was all grey even though she appeared to be smiling. She was dressed completely in black and I noticed that she still wore her wedding ring. I wanted to have her back with all my heart, for my mother was a comparative stranger to me and someone with whom I did not feel entirely at ease.

Despite living within the confines of Valencia, I was fully aware that there was a whole world beyond its boundaries and I used to ask my mother to teach me English so that I could adapt all the more quickly when she took me to London. I was sure she must speak the language after all her years away, but she was able to teach me only the most rudimentary words and phrases. In fact her English was virtually non-existent and even the postcards which she had sent to me written in Spanish had been scribbled by a friend. She liked to play the role of a long-suffering and underprivileged woman and she used her illiteracy as a weapon in her martyr's arsenal. I recall being somewhat puzzled as to how she managed to live and prosper in a country whose language she didn't speak. Even I had been able to speak good French after having lived with my uncle in France for only two years. Even so, I was able to reconcile all these things that didn't seem to add up and retained my blind faith in my mother, especially as I was convinced that she was getting ready to take me to England with her. Despite the wealth of evidence to the contrary, I still believed in the omnipotence of my parents.

My grandmother had finally gone to a better place, it had been explained to me, but I was still confused about my feelings. A part of me felt truly alone, heartbroken and lost, but another was excited about the prospect of going to England with my mother. As far as I knew, there was no one in Spain to look after me except my father, and she had made it very clear that in no way would she allow that to happen.

The second emotional bombshell in a period of weeks fell when I finally asked her about my accompanying her to England. 'No,' she said, shaking her head, 'it is impossible. You will have to stay in Spain, but I have to go back to London for my work. I don't know what to do with you. There is a possibility that two friends of mine in London can arrange for you to live with their brother and his wife in Asturias, in a town called Gijón. This couple are already looking after their grandson, Javier. He is two years older than you, and one more child will not be a great hardship to them. They say they can look after you for a short period while I sort myself out in London. I will send them money each month to keep you.' My heart was broken by this revelation; I felt devastated. It seemed to me that there was now no doubt at all that my mother didn't want me, my father wasn't rushing forward to claim me and my grandmother, in dying, had now left me utterly deserted. I begged and pleaded with my mother to take me to London, telling her how hard I would work at my studies and what a good girl I would be. But my efforts were wasted, for whatever incentives to my mother my ten-year-old brain was able to conjure up, she was able to counter them, employing the subtlest of emotional blackmail. Clearly annoyed by the inconvenience of the whole business, she set about making arrangements for my transfer to Asturias, all the time trying to cushion the blow by intimating that it would be for only a short period. It turned out to be six years.

The couple with whom I was to live were called Mercedes and Ramón. Mercedes came to fetch me, travelling down to Valencia from Gijón, an industrial port on the Atlantic coast in northern Spain. She looked like a typical Spanish countrywoman: fat and just as matriarchal as my grand-mother but with considerably more bitterness and without the blood bond which had held my grandmother and I together. From the moment she arrived in the flat, red-faced and puffing from the exertion of walking and carrying her bags, Mercedes showed little or no interest in me and certainly no sympathy for my plight. Even I was aware that I was a pretty little thing with long, dark-blonde hair and green eyes and a fairly ebullient personality. All this was completely lost on this particular bumpkin and I have a vague memory of her looking me up and down as if assessing whether or not I was going to prove expensive to feed and maintain. My mother and her were soon at loggerheads over a price for my maintenance. I am sure that to Mercedes it was no more than a business transaction, just as, with no emotions involved, she might to go market to buy a horse or purchase a dog from a neighbouring farm in exchange for chickens and vegetables.

Her priority seemed to be to make sure that all the financial terms were settled and that she was not being taken advantage of or at risk of finding herself out of pocket. During their conversations she would moan and shake her head as if my mother were putting too great a burden on her and expecting too much for the meagre compensation on offer. My mother would spread her hands in gestures of martyrdom and helplessness as if she had done all she was capable of and had offered as much as she could afford. I recall feeling that I was an unwanted nuisance to both of them: on the one hand a drain on my mother's resources, and on the other a great imposition on Mercedes. I was rather frightened and intimidated by the woman's impressive bulk as she towered over me, rough hands on her wide hips. Like a good number of women of her status and generation, she had a fairly formidable attitude, a weathered face and all the gentility and grace of an ill-tempered ox. It was obvious that she was not someone of whom I was going to grow fond.

From the moment Mercedes had arrived she had complained about everything, from the inconvenience and length of her journey while she felt unwell, to the weather and the excess of stairs to my mother's sixth-floor flat. She made it abundantly clear that taking me on was a phenomenal sacrifice, made because of her inherent goodwill and Christian duty, as well as a favour to her sisters-in-law in England. It seemed that there was not a bone, muscle or joint in her ample body which was not causing her pain, and it was all apparently brought on by the inconsiderate way in which other people expected her to look after their selfish needs and her efforts to get them out of difficult situations which were entirely of their own making. It seemed that I was to be just one more burden upon this corpulent figure and what with all the martyrdom that was flying around the room during the negotiations, I'm surprised that neither of them demanded instant canonization as part of the deal. My mother didn't seem to think that there was anything wrong with this attitude and I suppose she was just relieved to have found an answer to her problem, even if it was proving expensive. Towards the end, after an agreement had been reached, she was quite pleasant and polite to the woman who had made it possible for her to return to London, her dilemma resolved. In fact, at this time, my mother had little alternative but to find somewhere for me in Spain. Britain's immigration laws were strict, making it impossible for my mother to have had me with her if she had wanted to. In addition, I later learnt that her accommodation was no more than a bedsit and that she had little immediate prospect of getting anything bigger. But to a little girl who desperately wanted to be with her mother, words like 'impossible' are not impenetrable barriers that cannot be overcome by an apparently omnipotent parent. Thus, although I was convinced that my mother didn't want me with her, part of me felt that it was not entirely the truth.

When the deal had been struck and details of payment agreed, I left Valencia with Mercedes two days later, having received promises from my mother that this was only a temporary situation which, of course, I believed. My new guardian and I took the express train north-westwards to Madrid and then changed to a slow train heading due north to the industrial, mining and fishing communities centred around Asturias and Gijón on the Bay of Biscay. It must be remembered that regional differences in Spain, as in a number of European countries, are enormous: from lifestyle and food to language and culture. Although our way of life in Valencia had been relatively simple, it was still lived in a thriving and busy city where the streets were always crowded and people were going about their business of making money, enjoying themselves and getting on with their lives. It is impossible to live completely in the past in any city or town, however poor you may be. But in rural areas, far from the centres of culture and civilizing government, in some respects time can stand still for centuries. Attitudes, habits and deeply held beliefs can remain fixed, unchallenged and unyielding, ignorant views can be championed as eternal truths and all manner of unkindness and cruelty are sometimes excused on account of hardship. But I knew nothing of this. I knew only about the place which I was leaving, and only a child knows what the imagination can conjure up when journeying into the unknown in the company of a comparative stranger.

My mother had done a good job in convincing me that the new direction in which my life was turning was for the best and that she would call for me to join her in London as soon as possible. Thus, despite the recent loss of my grandmother, the inevitable flight back to England of my mother and my deluge of tears at her departure, I found the journey to Gijón an exciting experience. We spent two days on trains traversing the country and from the outset I was determined to make the most of the event. I certainly had no intention of sitting beside the abundant frame of Mercedes for the duration of the journey, just staring out of the window, and most probably she didn't want me there either. I decided instead, confident and affable child that I was, to explore the other carriages and meet the other people on board, for I was convinced that they would be as excited about such a monumental journey as I was. From what I remember, the other passengers were very kind and hospitable to the playful little girl with long pigtails running from compartment to compartment graciously introducing herself and chattering endlessly about everything that was going on. No doubt for many of them I made a pleasant distraction from the tedium of the journey. During that lengthy excursion some of my fellow travellers would share their food with me and ask me about myself, my unusual first name, which means 'welcome', and my ultimate destination.

When the train stopped in the little villages on the way through Segovia, Valladolid, León and the mountain range known as the Picos de Europa, women would get on selling hot crusty bread and cakes filling the carriages with the wonderful warm smells of their tempting wares and the sounds of their sales patter as they passed through the train. Other passengers produced fruit, cheeses and cold meats from their bags and hung their traditional Spanish water bottles out of the windows on ropes to keep them cold as we chugged on across the permanently snow-capped mountains.

Dawn broke as we passed between the peaks and the richness and variety of the view was quite breathtaking. The landscape was completely different from the flatlands of Valencia: immense, rugged and dramatic. It made me feel very small but also excited at the same time, even though Gijón, where I was going to live, was similar to many other towns to the east and west of it along the Mar Cantábrico. Mercedes, being more concerned about the fact that the uncomfortable seats were worsening whatever arthritic condition she decided was prevailing at that moment, was utterly indifferent to everything going on outside and grumbled constantly about the length of the journey.

I was missing my grandmother terribly and my mother as well, although as I look back now it is clear that it was more out of habit and principle than anything else. However, always the ambitious child and keen to resume my studies, I was determined to make the most of the situation. Therefore I convinced myself that I was going to a new family from where I would attend a new school and meet new and exciting friends. I made myself think of the journey as a huge adventure and actually found myself looking forward to seeing my new home, wondering what my room and family would be like and how I would get on with Javier, Mercedes and Ramón's grandson. Living in close proximity to a boy was going to be a novel experience and I wasn't too sure how I felt about it.

Gijón is a lively modern city originally built on the narrow Santa Catalina headland between two inlets, which today serve as harbour and beach, known as the Playa de San Lorenzo. Parts of the town are very elegant, with their smart late-seventeenth-century buildings, but as far as I know, one of its main claims to fame is that it was the birthplace of Gaspar Jovellanos, one of Spain's most eminent men of letters in the eighteenth century: poet, reformer, liberal economist, author and politician.

Mercedes, Ramón and their grandson Javier lived in a first-floor apartment in a community of homes built and run by the local workers themselves. My new playmate was about twelve and his father, also called Ramón, was separated from his wife and worked in Belgium. Javier had been left with his grandparents rather than his estranged mother, much as Rosita and I had been left with our grandmother. Mercedes and Ramón were probably in their early sixties. At some stage in their lives the elderly couple must have inherited a considerable amount of old furniture because the small rooms were cluttered and gloomy. My bedroom was nice enough, except for the bedstead, which was huge and dark with a giant carved eagle on the headboard. The creature used to glower down at me as if I were a small and edible rodent which it was about to pounce on and carry away in its sharp, hooked beak.

The older Ramón – there is a tedious tradition in Spain of employing the same first name for successive generations of the same family which causes considerable confusion when you are trying to identify the individuals in family sagas – had retired some time earlier from the building profession. On reflection I realize that he was a nice old man, much liked by everyone, and ready to help others whenever he could. He was, however, as are many Spanish men of that generation, living firmly under the thumb and watchful eye of his wife. Mercedes ran the household in a manner somewhere between that of a strict quartermaster and a mad, despotic ruler. Everyone had their chores and domestic duties to perform and woe betide anyone whose work wasn't up to scratch. From the day of my arrival Javier alone bore the physical brunt of her temper, but later she bore down on the two of us. Once again I was both witness to, and on the receiving end of, domestic violence. Indeed, for a long period of my life it was my sincere belief that this was part and parcel of daily family life and something to which I would eventually have to adapt.

There was a lovely dog in the household, a fat pointer bitch called Chispa, whom I grew to love. It was the beginning of my great love affair with dogs, although it would be many years before I was in a position to own one myself. Ramón was perhaps even softer about his hound than I was and even allowed her to sleep on the bed with him. She in turn was completely devoted to her master and although I played with her in the flat, she would never go outside with anyone but the old man.

My new home was on the outskirts of Gijón, in a modern complex of council-type blocks surrounded by fields and countryside in which, when not at school or busy with domestic chores and homework, I was quite happy to wander alone in complete safety. I settled in at school with great ease and, as I had expected, made many new friends. My school and education were my life and something on which I was able to focus. This was not because I believed that through diligence and hard work I would one day be able to develop beyond the parameters of a safe if dull life as a Spanish citizen, but because I was naturally intelligent and eager to learn; though it must be said that I never found school work inordinately hard. At this stage of my life, from the age of ten to around fifteen, I was not possessed of any grandoise plans to conquer the world. It was my intention to go to university and enter a worthy profession such as the law.

To say that Mercedes was not easy to live with is a delightful under-statement, although the first two years of my sojourn in Asturias were comparatively happy and relaxed. Nevertheless, from the outset it was quite clear that she had the ability to be incredibly cruel and unkind. The young Javier had a problem with bedwetting, a not uncommon problem in some families, and Mercedes used to make the poor boy wear his soiled underpants on his head in the morning after an 'accident', for all the neighbours to see. I know now that the problem is sometimes hereditary but even at that young age I could see that what the woman was doing was both ignorant and likely to make his problem worse and not better. But she was not a woman to whom I would have ever dared express my views and in any case she would not have taken any notice. Furthermore, I always risked getting a smack around the head for my troubles.

Javier and I got on very well, not out of sympathy on my part but because he was intelligent and alert and we shared a common bond in that we had both been more or less abandoned by our parents. The adults around us never seemed to consider for one moment that our having been forsaken by close family and suffering the wrath of Mercedes would have any detrimental effect on us, and so they had no idea just how much we were hurting inside. To them we probably appeared as little more than barely tolerable responsibilities.

Both Ramón and Mercedes, owing to their advancing years, were permanently under the impression that they were ill with something or other. I suspect that most of their problems stemmed from their appalling diet, for the food we ate was rather primitive in nutritional terms, full of fats, oils and sugars. I recall being sent shopping for the family and often having to queue for hours in the local market to get a good cut of meat. On occasion, because I was trusting and respectful, one of the shopkeepers would fob me off with a piece of meat that Mercedes would consider inferior, and she would hit me about the head with her fist until my ears rang in order to teach me to do better next time. Of course, what she did was very wrong but, without excusing her in any way, I suspect that it was simply an incidence of repressed frustration, continuing an ugly and ignorant tradition. Whenever I cried, which I always did on such occasions, my tears seemed to infuriate her all the more.

The old man and Chispa the dog used to go shooting in the local countryside and would return with grotesque braces of dead birds which Mercedes would display on a towel on my bed, beneath the steely gaze of the carved eagle. I was terrified of all the blood, but if I showed any fear she would pick up one of the dead birds and smack me in the face with it, saying, 'That'll give you something to be frightened of!' Perhaps in her own way she was trying to build up my character, or maybe I simply got on her nerves. Along with all the other verbal abuse, I found it utterly soul-destroying.

After sorting out the birds Mercedes would stand and admire them before hanging them in the larder. She would then make a point of sending me in there every time she deemed it appropriate, and as I groped around in the darkness I could feel the feathers from the suspended carcasses brushing against my face. I hated it, and her, and tried to get out of the house as much as possible to be alone or with my friends.

Mercedes used to take pleasure in hurting and insulting me. 'Your mother doesn't love you,' she used to say whenever I displeased her, which seemed to be most of the time. 'That is why you are here. And her payments never come on time. If they don't arrive more promptly you will be put out on the street to earn your living the hard way, which you probably wouldn't be any good at anyway. You are very lucky to be here with us because we are kind and compassionate people, otherwise you would have nowhere to go. You will never amount to anything in your life. You are a nobody, a nothing, an unwanted child!'

Even as an adult it isn't always easy to stand up against anyone who chooses to demean, insult and verbally abuse you. When you are a child of under sixteen it is virtually impossible. There is also the possibility that if an adult systematically berates and belittles you frequently enough, the words end up penetrating deep into your subconscious. Such was the case with Mercedes' endless tirades. I began to find myself thinking that what she was saying must be true as nothing I seemed to do was up to standard and that perhaps she was indeed right and I was the worthless individual she accused me of being. She certainly seemed to be right in one aspect: that no one in my family had seen fit to take me into their care and that therefore I must be unlovable. Her onslaught over, I would at first become frustrated by my own inability to fight back. But then my anger would convince me that, despite my age and apparent ineffectuality, I did have some self-worth, was a better person than all her haranguing implied and that a time would come when I would no longer have to tolerate verbal and physical abuse from anyone.

It was while I was in Gijón that I was first introduced to television. To begin with it was just a black-and-white set belonging to some neighbours, around which we would gather at weekends. I was mesmerized by the flickering screen and it reminded me of my visits to the cinema in Valencia with my grandmother. Later Mercedes and Ramón acquired their own set and I was able to enjoy more diverse programmes than the badly dubbed films we used to watch with our neighbours. It is certainly true that it was television that brought home to me the rich panoply of lifestyles that existed outside of Spain and perhaps, in some small way, that old flickering set sowed in me the seeds of ambition that were ultimately to grow into such an exotic harvest. What I saw was a world into which I might be able to escape from the virtual prison sentence I was at that time suffering. Moreover, I continued to yearn for the day when my mother would ask me to join her in the teeming and opulent metropolis that was London.

She did visit me once in the six years I was in Gijón but we clashed when she tried to impose her will on me over how I dressed and wore my hair. She stayed for about three weeks but seemed more preoccupied with seeking the company of the younger Ramón, who had temporarily returned from Belgium.

It was while watching *The Man from U.N.C.L.E.*, featuring the heroes Napoleon Solo and Ilya Kuriakin, on the family's old television set, that I had the questionable pleasure of my first period. I remember that it was 16 April 1969 – curious how that date stuck in my mind – and I was twelve years old. I was absolutely terrified that I was about to bleed to death and I remember Mercedes packing me off to bed, as if that would have made any difference, telling me that from then on it was something that was going to happen to me every month. She totally failed to explain what was happening, so I was still terrified, and it was only later, from my school friends, that I learnt what was going on.

As my schooling progressed I became increasingly aware of the outside world, of the benefits of a sound education and the opportunities that would inevitably present themselves to those with the benefit of good academic qualifications. I soon outgrew the first school to which I was sent in Gijón and was granted a government sponsored scholarship to study for my *bachillerato* at a more advanced local school.

On Sundays the household went off diligently to church. We would all dress up in our best clothes and from our pew I would see other girls of my age and older in a variety of pretty dresses and hairstyles. I remember envying them in that every Sunday they seemed to have a different outfit, whereas I was rather limited in my wardrobe. It wasn't a malevolent envy, merely that I too wanted to have a wide selection of beautiful clothes. In the event, whatever sartorial inadequacies I may have felt at that stage of my life, I more than compensated for later on. Because I was considered responsible and bright, I used to help teach the young children their catechisms after mass at Sunday school. The school was run by the Jesuits, and the children, most of them seven or eight years old, were obliged to learn their gospels and stories of the life of Jesus in order to prepare for their first communion, as I had in Valencia in 1965. The responsibility of such a task made me feel very grown-up and important. At the same time I was also finding in my school work an escape from the misery of an increasingly unhappy home life. My teachers had great expectations of me and it was already assumed that I would be going to university, most probably to read law. I enjoyed the praise that my tutors heaped on me and greedily lapped up their encouragement and support. Sometimes, if one of the staff was absent, I would be asked to teach some of the smaller children. I felt very proud to be asked and even more proud when a little boy or girl recognized me in the street and called me 'Miss'. For the first time in my life I began to feel more like an adult and less the hopeless miscreant that I was treated as at home.

I remember there being four girls in my class, including myself, who were considered brighter and more competent than the rest, and we became very competitive and envious of one another. We were always struggling to be first in every subject and competed vigorously for the attention of the teachers. Despite the rivalry, one of the girls, Reyes, who later went to live in Venezuela, became my best friend and occasionally I would accompany her home after school. For a reason which I have not yet been able to fathom, her mother was also unpleasant to me at times, telling me that my mother didn't love me and that was why I was in Asturias. Then one day, after I had stubbornly spent hours defending my mother and telling everyone how special she was, she came to visit me at school. I recall running over to her and shouting very loudly, 'Mama! Mama!' This was to show to my friends that she really did exist and that she was as beautiful as I had made her out to be and obviously cared for me, after all, having come all the way from England to see me.

Perhaps because I was so terribly unhappy living with Mercedes and Ramón, my exam results were not quite as good as they might have been. However, I had now reached the age of fifteen and was obliged to leave secondary school. I felt certain that my mother would now invite me to be with her in London but, once again, I was disappointed. Actually, she didn't know what to do with me, whether to leave me in Spain so that I could retake the few subjects in which I hadn't quite succeeded, or take me to London. Naturally I was deeply saddened when she failed to grab the opportunity to have me with her, but in her indecision I saw a glimmer of hope. She might not have been desperate to have me but before long her indecision would be great enough for me to have some prevailing influence over her. As a delaying tactic she moved me back to Valencia, to a boarding-school run by nuns where I could retake my exams. Actually it was more of a convent and for the six months I was there I was perhaps more consciously unhappy than at any other time. Forbidden to have any contact with my father or his family, I hated the regime, which I found dreadfully restrictive, I made no friends at all and loathed the fact that once again I was being treated like a prisoner, along with all of the other children, most of whom were orphans. I was truly unhappy even though there were some aspects of my time there that were not too unpleasant. I learnt embroidery, at which we would spend hours while listening to the radio, and I recall very much preferring my kitchen chores to the laundry duty, which I hated.

My mother, who came to Valencia once during my time at the convent, had a boyfriend, a chauffeur called Julian. She allowed him to use the flat where I used to live with my grandmother and which she still kept. She told me that she was in love with him, but I never liked him and infuriated her by refusing to ask him how he was when we all went out. As she was in London nearly all of the time she told me that I should look upon him as my father and let him take me out. The thought of this man replacing my father disgusted me. He tried to impress me by arriving in his Mercedes to take me out but I began to realize that he appeared to use every opportunity and excuse to touch my body, running his hands over my breasts and legs. It was an extremely unpleasant sensation for a young girl who had absolutely no experience of the opposite sex.

I told the Mother Superior that I didn't want to go out with Julian any more because of his approaches. She was very comforting and understanding and agreed to deny him access to me but was obliged to write to my mother to explain why she had taken such action.

The next time my mother came to Valencia she exploded at me. 'You are just jealous of my happiness,' she screamed, 'you will do anything to ruin my chances in life!' I simply did not know what to say or how to answer back, so I just lowered my eyes submissively and allowed her to berate me until her temper had finally exhausted itself. Needless to say, Julian was soon replaced in her affections by someone new and equally temporary.

I was now sixteen and realized that my mother would soon no longer be able to force me to do as she wanted and that I would ultimately be making my own decisions. I was anxious to make the right choices and asked the daughter of the housekeeper at the convent to sneak into the school chapel, where we were not really allowed to go other than at specified times. She was to slip my mother's wedding ring, which she'd given to me, on to the finger of the effigy of the Virgin Mary. Then she was to ask on my behalf for guidance, for which I also prayed most urgently. Should I stay in Spain and continue my studies there or should I take a leap into the unknown and insist on going to London with my mother, now that the immigration laws had been somewhat relaxed?

I chose to head for London, that mythical and wondrous city full of promise about which I had fantasized so hard and so long. It was to be my first flight and the moment I boarded the plane I could feel my heart pounding in my chest as I embarked on a journey which was to alter the course of my life beyond all recognition.

3

A Glimpse of the Possible

*I*arrived in London at the end of 1972 and it should have been the fulfilment of all my dreams – and in a way it was. At the same time my arrival at my mother's residence finally shattered all my illusions about her being the grand and wonderful woman I had always allowed myself to believe she was. In no time at all I realized that a good deal of the nasty things her sister Francisca, and occasionally my grandmother and others, had said about her were true. In my fantasies she had been this unimpeachable and elegant woman who was always arriving or leaving on aeroplanes with glamorous luggage. Her clothes had always seemed so much better than anyone else's and she would smell of exotic soaps and perfumes, small samples of which she used to bring me as a child. She always appeared, on her infrequent visits to Spain, like a modern city woman descending among simpler people, and during her short stays I could never get enough of her seemingly sophisticated and elevated ways.

In the dull grey world of reality she was working as a housekeeper for the Sheppard Trust's home for elderly and retired gentlewomen in Lansdowne Walk, Notting Hill, living in staff accommodation. I had been able to join her finally because my mother, whose spoken English was very poor, had approached the Trust's secretary, a kind lady called Elizabeth, about her daughter. In turn it was the patron of the trust, Lord Hastings, who sponsored my immigration. There was certainly nothing wrong with the job or the place, although it was certainly not how I imagined my mother living. What was most upsetting was the fact that she obviously found my presence a burden and wasn't exactly pleased at having me around. Of course, my mother's attitude towards me should have long ago been obvious, but a child will do anything to avoid facing the truth of being unwanted and unloved. Despite all the evidence I had witnessed of her indifference to me over the years, I had still managed to convince myself that she had stayed away purely because she had been obliged to do so. I had believed it when everyone had told me that she had had to go to London in order to work and that I couldn't join her for legal reasons. I chose to accept that she was as unhappy about us being separated as I was but that the situation was beyond her control. But now I had seen how easy it was for me to board a plane and fly to England, and I was facing the undeniable fact that she had not exactly been living for the moment when we could be reunited. Obviously she had been dreading it. I was made to feel that I was an unwelcome intrusion into her life, limiting her ability to act as a free agent. Moreover, I was acutely aware that she was making no effort at all to get to know her teenage daughter.

She had a long-term boyfriend, Paul Munchenbach, who was a little older than her. He was an Englishman of Alsatian descent and was certainly kind enough to me when I first arrived in London. He worked in a greengrocer's and used to bring us fruit and vegetables. As well as her job at the retirement home, my mother worked every Thursday as a part-time lady's maid and seamstress to Lady Edith Foxwell, taking care of her clothes. I had no idea about titles and the class structure in England but to have a maid purely to look after one's clothes seemed frightfully grand and I was rather intrigued by such people. Once I had got to know the seven or eight ladies who lived in the home, they gradually usurped my mother as people to whom to look up and respect now that the pedestal was vacant. They were gentle, well-spoken and kind, and the sort of people I could admire.

To stem my endless questions about style and manners, my mother, who was always one to encourage my professional ambitions, used to pass on little etiquette tips like always sending thank-you notes for everything. I never forgot anything she told me as I wanted to learn all the rules of this new society so that if and when my opportunity arose, I would be able to behave correctly and with decorum. It was rather like peeking through the curtains into a new and mystical environment populated by people the like of whom I had never encountered before. At this stage of my life I certainly had no social or financial ambitions and knew little of the ways of the world. I was a normal, healthy girl with an agile mind, keen to impress my elders and justifiably curious about and intrigued by everyone and everything around me. My mother was learning from the residents as well, always dressing smartly in suits and high heels and never looking the part of a housekeeper and cook. I particularly remember that she had an astrakhan coat which I thought was the most elegant garment I had ever seen.

Everything about London as a city excited me and from what I could tell it was not at all different from the postcards I had received over the years, ostensibly from my mother. On my first Sunday in London I was taken on a sightseeing tour of such places as Regent Street, Piccadilly Circus, Trafalgar Square and the Houses of Parliament. Lamentably, it was not my mother who took me. Old Ramón from Gijón, whose dog I had loved so much, had two sisters in London, both working in domestic employment. In fact it was they, Amparo and Ramona, who had first suggested to my mother that their brother and his wife Mercedes might be prepared to take care of me after the death of my grandmother. Amparo, the younger of the two, was the one who kindly took me on a bus tour of the capital's sights. I was absolutely mesmerized. The buildings were both grander and bigger than anything I had ever seen and I wandered around staring and open-mouthed whenever the bus stopped to take in a particular sight. It was the first time that I had ever seen a black man and Amparo was careful to teach me that they were called 'coloured gentleman' and not 'Negroes'. I remember thinking that it was all a far cry from Valencia and Gijón and that if I was to remain anywhere in the future it was going to be London.

However, I still needed to finish my studies before I could make my own way in this seemingly most grown-up of cities and over the next couple of years the confusing mists of my childhood fantasies, illusions and dreams began to clear, affording me a better vision of what I wanted to do with my life.

It is to be remembered that at the age of sixteen or seventeen, one's goals and lifetime ambitions are still in their infancy and enjoying one's youth, with its multitude of distractions, seems paramount. Only later is one able to prioritize one's life. Even though I knew that my studies were essential to my being able to advance professionally, I was still not sure exactly what I wanted to do. The adult part of me still wanted to be a lawyer but the more youthful side still yearned to be like that famous Spanish teen idol Marisol. I loved the academic side of school, studying and taking exams, and I definitely wanted to do something that would make use of my quick and active brain. And like any other teenager, I was fascinated by movie stars and stage actresses, who seemed such beautiful and glamorous women, wore beautiful clothes and were adored by all. There was a totally understandable side of me – the little girl who had been shunted around always trying to win approval of those around her – that wanted to partake of the elegance and charisma of such people and for once be on the receiving end of some well-deserved adulation.

My mother's accommodation consisted of just three rooms: a kitchen, bathroom and a bedroom, which doubled as a sitting-room. In fact even the kitchen was not entirely private, as it was in there that she not only prepared meals for us two but also the daily lunches for the resident ladies of the home. My bed was one of those disguised as a bookcase which you could pull down from the wall in the area which acted as a dining-room for the residents. Only one meal was served per day and the ladies would let my mother know individually whether or not they would be eating. As for their breakfast and dinners, these were not really our concern as most of them had social lives and their small apartments in the home each boasted a kitchenette. There was a pretty garden at the back to which everyone had access, and initially I thought that sharing my life there with my mother could make me happy. I was determined to win her love, to show her just what a benefit having a daughter like me could mean, and I was willing to do anything to please her. During the day I attended the nearby Ladbroke Upper School, where I was studying for my O levels, having picked up English with consummate ease, and at night I went to a college in Gloucester Road, South Kensington, to continue my studies. The workload was considerable but my mother was adamant that I should do as much as I could in order to ensure that, unlike her, I would never have to endure the ignominy of working just to earn money. She told me that I was in London to study and that that was what I should do. In that respect she was very good, even paying for me to do a course in computer programming and data processing during my summer breaks.

As time went on my mother's attitude towards me became more and more impossible. I realize now that there was a strong feeling of jealousy coming from her as I made further and further progress scholastically and had obviously surpassed her in terms of intellect some way back, although this was certainly nothing I lauded over her. She felt threatened by my looks and confidence and it came to the point where she could no longer bear to see me happy or enjoying life.

Her feelings towards me manifested themselves in one of three ways. On occasion – for example, when I took something from the fridge without her permission, was late home, or had put on a little make-up – she would be very angry. Later she took to locking me out of the flat for hours on end, but no matter how hard I tried I was always on the receiving end of the 'silent treatment'. Some days I would wake up early in order to make a little breakfast for both of us, preparing all the things which I knew she liked, only to find that she was not talking to me. We would then continue in silence for the time when I was not at school, with me pleading with her to speak and she just staring past me as if I didn't exist.

On one occasion I was locked out in the garden and was so distraught that I started to cry my eyes out. One of the old ladies, who had the nicest apartment with a terrace overlooking the garden, noticed me from the first floor and came down to see what the problem was. I was unable to stop myself from pouring out my unhappiness and told her that my mother had locked me out, ending with a wail of, 'And I am so hungry.'

'Dear me,' she tutted, 'what a naughty thing to do.' I thought that was such an English thing to say. She very sweetly took me up to her beautiful room, giving me tea and looked after me until my mother came home and unlocked the door.

Sometimes my mother would use the lock on the old fridge to stop me getting access to it, not because I was overweight but out of sheer malice and vindictiveness. It became hell on earth for me and I desperately longed to be independent of her, to no longer be beholden to her for anything, to not have to listen to her cruel jibes and endure her constant rejection. Some days she made me just want to die because I couldn't understand what it was that I had done to offend or upset her. At one point I had been so happy at the prospect of being with her and now I was working as hard as I could to be a model student in order to make her proud of me. I was desperately hurt when she acted as if she hated me, especially since, because of her limited numerical abilities, I was taking care of the household accounts for the Trust. I wanted to show her that I intended to be successful and make my own way in life and had no intention of continuing to depend on her for financial support any longer than was absolutely necessary.

Despite my initial impression of Paul, my mother's long-standing boyfriend, as a fairly decent man, he ultimately proved to be no different from any of the other men I had known in my life. Their relationship was turbulent and he often either turned up drunk or became drunk at our little flat, where he would occasionally spend the night. They would shout and scream insults at one another and argue violently about the money he was giving her. On one occasion, after a particularly heavy bout of drinking, he set about the two of us with fists flying. The following morning, even though my mother had asked me not to, I went down and reported the incident to the police at Ladbroke Grove Police Station, where I was told that if it happened again they would take Paul in and caution him. Needless to say, the two of them made up their differences, as they usually did, and despite continuing acrimonious rows, he later moved into the little flat after I had left. When his father died he inherited a house in Chiswick and he and my mother lived there together.

The elderly ladies who lived in the home were charming to me and I would frequently take refuge in their rooms, talking with them when my mother had banished me into silence. Most of them were extremely elegant, having led fabulously glamorous lives before coming to the home. They were all either widowed or unmarried and continued to lead productive and comfortable lives of their own. I was determined to listen to their every story and recollection, hungry to hear tales of their gilded youth and of more frivolous times. There was one lady in particular whom I used to visit. Lady Edith Bird had been a great society lady but was now in her late sixties, the widow of a well-known judge and still surprisingly active. Her room was tidy, smelt of lavender and was full of old photographs and personal mementoes. The table was always set for two people even though she had been on her own for a long period of time. I dare say it was an eccentricity in memory of her late husband.

Lady Bird often used to go out with young army officers, most probably the sons of friends, or younger nephews, and grandchildren, who used to call and pick her up. I used to read to her for hours on end and ask her all sorts of questions about herself and life in England. In turn, she would tell me about issues of interest to women and I soaked up every bit of information she gave me, no matter how trivial and insignificant it seemed.

By the age of eighteen, although I was still a little uncertain as to what

I wanted to do, I was convinced of one fact: I most definitely wanted to be different from all the women I had known as a child in Spain. I wanted to extend myself beyond their limited achievements, experience more than domestic and marital servitude with all the implications which that role entailed. I intended to escape from all the rejection, malice and aggression which had filled my world and had no intention of growing old full of disappointment, unresolved ambition and the resentment of others more fortunate than me. No longer for me the bitterness, regrets over opportunities lost and disillusionment of my childhood.

Although Lady Edith was very much older than me she would take me to events like garden parties at her friends' houses in elegant, established residential areas like the Boltons and Belgravia. I even accompanied her on a number of occasions to afternoon tea at the House of Lords, where the women were extremely well dressed, their hats and gloves like those worn by characters I had seen in the cinema in Valencia and the flickering black-and-white television in Gijón. I learnt from her how to behave in polite society, how to make conversation and how to thank people for their kindness and hospitality. She was Professor Higgins to my Eliza Doolittle, apart from the fact that there was no challenge involved and she received nothing for her efforts, which came purely from the heart. She was a most charming and lovely lady, to whom I shall always be grateful. At one stage she introduced me to a friend of hers living in Pembridge Villas, a lady who agreed to improve my spoken English at weekends, and I would happily go to her house to read to her and practise my speech exercises.

Lady Edith was a member of a conservative group called the Primrose League, which, she told me, had been established by one of the great prime ministers of the Victorian era, Benjamin Disraeli. Here she introduced me as her 'young friend' to ministers of the day such as Peter Walker and Sir Alec Douglas-Home. Still in my late teens, I couldn't help but be impressed by these dignified, educated and gently spoken men, the foundations of British society and a far cry from the loud and boorish men, my father apart, I had encountered in my childhood.

'Bienvenida,' Lady Edith said to me one day, 'you have to succeed with your life and with being a woman. You must have someone who can look after you and protect you, someone who will be kind to you and give you security.' I felt at the time that I knew what she was talking about. I was only too well aware from my own bitter experience what the lack of these things meant, but I was still far too young and innocent to act on her well-meaning advice. She was from a generation and class who expected these things from their husbands when they married and now, with the benefit of hindsight, I feel flattered that, despite the obvious disparity in our respective status, she felt this to be a piece of information of which I should and could make use. Later I was to form my own views on the subject of marriage and relationships, although sadly most of them were based on my experiences as a child and the behaviour of a few men whom I was to meet over the years.

In spending time with Lady Edith, which I thoroughly enjoyed, I had glimpsed a world very different from the one I might have expected to enter, given my relatively humble beginnings. And I certainly didn't hanker after a more elevated and lofty lifestyle or crave the company of educated, cultured and prosperous individuals. I was too young for that. But I was acutely aware that in order to feel relaxed and confident enough to move in such circles, should the opportunity ever arise, I would need to educate myself further, improve my mind and develop and then nurture my own image. Only in this way would I be able to deal with these refined people as equals and not behave like some parvenu or unknown who had emerged from comparative obscurity. I was still at an age where I needed the comfort and security of a home life but also there was a growing awareness within me that to be pretty and amusing was not enough if I was truly to make a success of my life. I needed to have more to offer as there were too many other girls with those assets, and I realized that I was going to have to work very hard to raise myself above the rest if I was to end up as someone of significance and standing.

At the age of eighteen I was impatient to get out of the rut of adolescence and put the whole of my childhood behind me. I had passed all of my exams and felt ready to leave school. I wanted very much to be independent of everyone and did not feel that, despite having the opportunity to do so, I would have the patience to spend the next few years at university, existing on next to no money and returning to my mother's home in the holidays. I decided that I would find other, less formal and time-consuming ways to continue my education and broaden my horizons.

I still felt a considerable loyalty and devotion to my mother and so I felt that my first priority should be to get a job, not only to gain a degree of independence for myself but also to help my mother out financially as much as I could. I had come top of my class in the course on computer sciences, so this seemed like the best place to start. Armed with this qualification, as well as a few others and two and a half spoken languages, I applied for and got a full-time position at the London School of Hygiene and Tropical Medicine, a part of London University. My department was based in Bedford Square, where I was working as an assistant statistician in the data-processing section. It was a fascinating time, not only because of the diversity of the work but also because during my lunch breaks I would go to the library to read or to the lecture halls and listen to the doctors delivering their lectures to the students. I enjoyed my work, made a few friends and loved the access which my work gave me to so much learning.

Best of all, perhaps, I was earning a salary for the first time in my life and taking the first tentative steps towards being independent and in control of my future. I felt immensely proud to be able to go home and give money to my mother and delighted to be able to buy myself make-up and clothes without having to ask her permission or rely on her hand-outs. I was so ravenous for experience and knowledge that I wanted to work all the time, weekends included. I couldn't wait to get back to the office and away from home, always fretful and impatient if I wasn't constantly improving myself, and eager to escape from the domain where my mother still ruled with her difficult moods. When I was working alone in a library or office I was in complete control and that felt deeply satisfying. I was aware that if I bided my time and made the right decisions, nothing and no one could stop me fulfilling my potential. I just needed time to grow and a few lucky breaks which, I was sure, would provide the necessary opportunities.

Like most girls of my age I was very aware of all the images that filled fashion magazines of the ideal woman – 'Reading dreams' as Truman Capote describes glossy magazines in *Breakfast at Tiffany's*. I could see, from watching on television and the cinema the women and film stars whom I admired, that all those years of oily fried food in Spain had left me a little plumper than I should have been. I had formed in my mind a strong image of how I wanted to look and what I wanted to become, and I was sure that I could achieve it. It was very clear to me that clothing and a slim body were crucial to any woman who wanted to be glamorous. I did not waste my time being jealous and envying the women I saw who were slim. I simply knew that I could achieve the same look with hard work. Having mastered English, passed all my exams and now making good progress at work, I knew what hard work was all about and was determined to apply the same efforts to losing those extra pounds and the layer of puppy fat that I still carried around with me. In the School's library there was a big section devoted to books on human nutrition and soon I had become completely obsessed with the subject, reading every article and scientific report about it. I learnt the calorific value of virtually all known edible substances and knew exactly what foods had what consequences on the body. What I didn't know was that all the effort and dedication which I was directing at my diet was an emotional transference, a way of avoiding my unhappiness at home and my lack of security and stability.

I had always been very fond of food and I knew that it was going to be very hard to cut down on all the things that I loved. These were inevitably the most fattening things, such as chocolate, puddings and other treats, which I consumed mostly as a substitute for emotional comfort, although I must admit that I have always had a sweet tooth. But I was determined to prove to myself and perhaps others too that I was strong enough to deny myself things that I really enjoyed in order to achieve something that I wanted. My diet became a substitute for all the frustrations and disillusionment from which I still suffered. In addition, I felt that I had to show myself that I could overcome any short-term temptation that might be put before me in order to improve my chances of succeeding in life at some unknown point in the future. When you are unhappy it is only too easy to seek comfort and consolation by satisfying one's appetite, whether it be sexual, alcoholic or Epicurean, whereas it is often an emotional appetite that is really in need of attention. I knew that if I did not gain control of myself and my appetites I would be letting myself down, so I had to conquer my need for food.

At the end of *Breakfast at Tiffany's* the Holly Golightly character, played by Audrey Hepburn in the film version, discards her cat to show that she can overcome emotional dependence, that she is strong enough to stand on her own two feet without emotional crutches. I have always wanted to prove much the same thing, and controlling my consumption of food was the first stage. Only years later did I begin to understand that reliance on emotional support from the right person or people is not necessarily a sign of weakness but a sign of great strength and confidence. But I knew nothing of that then and I needed to be sure that I could achieve anything I wanted to and make whatever sacrifices were necessary in order to develop total self-reliance and control. As my life progressed there were to be many other opportunities for me to test my will-power in this way.

I cut out all soft drinks and confectionery of any kind and stopped picking at food between meals. I removed all fat from my diet, which was far too drastic a step, and for two years, during which time my periods stopped completely, all I ate was small amounts of steamed vegetables and fruit. I felt immensely proud of myself for the steely determination which I found in my character. I had truly believed that I could do it and now I was proving it. My weight dropped to below seven stone and I began to lose all my energy. I found that I was unable to keep my body warm and didn't even have the energy to sleep at night. My mother, who clearly knew I was suffering, insisted on keeping all the windows open at night, no matter how cold it was. Shivering and weak, I lay in bed watching the clock's minute hand as it slowly made its way round to the time when I would be obliged to get up and drag myself into work.

Fortunately the doctors at the School of Hygiene and Tropical Medicine could see what was happening. I had become anorexic. My hair and nails had grown weak and brittle and my skin was flaky from lack of natural oils. It must have been obvious that I was not well and could not do justice to my work. All I could think about was getting through the day and back home to bed so that I could pride myself on having gone yet one more day without food.

When I got home I would get into a hot bath, partly to get away from my mother, who was for ever on the prowl in a foul mood, and partly in a vain attempt to raise my body temperature. The doctors with whom I worked very kindly and understandingly gave me day-releases to see a Professor of Human Nutrition at University College Hospital, so that I could talk about the problem. I was amazed and impressed by how caring and supportive they were and it was to me a further confirmation of my belief that England was a wonderful country in which to live. No one had genuinely been concerned about my health since my grandmother had died in Valencia and even she had never really had the time to consider anything other than the most obvious and superficial symptoms. These people, however, really cared, more than even my mother, and I was deeply touched by all their concern and efforts.

The professor was extremely helpful to me, showing me that fundamentally it was a psychological problem rather than a physical disorder. 'You need to build your confidence,' she explained. 'You see, denying yourself food is really only showing strength of character and determination. Well, now you have proved that you can do it, so have the strength to decide not to harm your health any further and work out a healthier regime by which to live.'

She showed me what I was doing wrong and I gradually built up my diet in a disciplined and scientific manner, ensuring that I received the correct doses of vitamins and minerals by eating fish, cheese, vegetables, fruit and salad. I still wanted to be slim and she understood that. She convinced me that I could achieve the shape I wanted much more easily if I was eating sensibly and, after making a full recovery, I have, for the past twenty years, maintained my weight at within a couple of pounds either side of eight stone. But I know for a fact that, for my height, I should actually be about a stone heavier. I am certain that I haven't lost my sweet tooth, but by simply keeping to a carefully balanced diet and not allowing myself to fall into bad habits or indulge myself in moments of weakness, I have taught myself to dispel immediately any ideas of giving in to temptation. The irony is that much later on in my life I was to marry a man who turned out to be a fabulous cook.

Despite the big step forward of getting myself a good job with a steady income, my relationship with my mother grew no better and, as a result, I found it impossible to be happy with my life. I was a very solitary and reclusive figure, often depressed, and there were many times when I just wanted to die in order to escape the dull ache of misery which seemed permanently to fill my body. I did have some friends in the office but I had no social life to speak of at home and spent a lot of time watching television. In fact, this was not such a bad thing as I made a point of watching both serious and a few frivolous programmes and so was able to expand my understanding of politics and world events very considerably. I had tremendous mood swings which went from wild optimism and excitement about a life that might lie ahead of me to a bleak all-consuming sadness at my inability to get on with my mother – the very person with whom I felt I should have been closest. When I thought realistically about the future, all I could see was years of toil and hard work before I could be independent of her and possibly achieve some eminence in a chosen profession. Only at that point would I be able to move with confidence and pride in any social circle I chose.

I kept thinking about Lady Bird's advice and about the sort of life that I wanted and the type of woman I wanted to be. Most of all I longed to be fully independent, which I knew meant having money, in fact much more money than I was ever likely to earn if I carried on along a traditional career path. My salary was very rewarding to have, but I had only to do a little window-shopping in Bond Street to see that it was not going to get me even close to the sort of quality lifestyle that I wanted. There seemed to me to be an unbelievable and impossible chasm between the reality of my monthly pay cheque and the sort of money necessary to fund an elegant apartment of my own and all the accoutrements inseparable from that dream. No matter how hard I tried or what schemes I came up with, I could not see how to bridge that chasm.

The problem taxed my thoughts continually as I kept turning over Lady Bird's words in my head: 'You need to find a husband to look after you.' It was gradually becoming clear to me that I had two options. I could either work for years and years scrimping and saving to achieve an eventual financial reward, by which time I would probably be dead or too decrepit to enjoy it; or I could look for a short cut. The only short cut which I could envisage was to find a man who had already made a fortune and to use that relationship as a basis for meeting other successful people so as to further my career and gain the knowledge necessary to make a fortune of my own.

Although the second plan seemed to me by far the more attractive, I didn't like the idea of marrying someone. Not only because my experience with men was non-existent but because it seemed to defeat the whole purpose of trying to be independent and would actually result in me being just as dependent on another person as I had been as a child and in my teenage years. There had to be a better way, I was sure, of using my intelligence and abilities in a businesslike way in order to achieve the same results without the many penalties that I imagined were inherent in marriage. At that point in my life I had a fairly cynical and warped view of matrimony which stemmed mostly from the marriages and relationships that I had witnesses as a child in Spain and as an adolescent in London. They seemed to encompass everything I disliked most: domestic violence, heavy bouts of drinking, deceit, the break-up of the relationship to the detriment of the children involved and the gradual decline of physical, emotional and financial well-being.

Over time my mind worked constantly on the problem and I gradually developed a philosophy which was to become the basis of all my future successes. I decided to look upon myself as a one-woman business and, according to my newly evolved philosophy, I began to review my assets. I was quite pleased with the way I looked and was growing used to receiving compliments on my way of dressing and my femininity. But more important than anything else, I knew that I had a good brain. Not only was I clever, but I was also capable of working hard to improve myself, as I had amply demonstrated with the radical changes in my diet and my long working hours. As a one-woman business I had to develop a marketing plan and a clever, carefully thought out business strategy, using my quick and agile mind and a few feminine wiles that I knew I possessed even though they were not yet fully honed.

Perhaps unwittingly, Lady Edith had set me on the right track, but I intended to surpass any of her expectations. It was my intention to familiarize myself with everything there was to learn about the business of impressing and appealing to influential and affluent men, and that meant gathering information from every possible source. I made a point of watching all the great film stars of the past, determined to learn everything about the way they handled themselves: people like Bette Davis, Marlene Dietrich and Barbara Stanwyck.

I realized that these were neither pretty nor beautiful women in the classic sense, but they all had the type of beauty which imbued them with power. They had the courage to be themselves. Marlene Dietrich, for instance, was the first woman to wear a man's dinner suit and kiss another woman on the lips on film. Logically, it should have ended her career as a sexual icon but it achieved just the opposite, marking her out as a woman strong, confident and brazen enough to please herself. She had incredible sexual power but she never took her clothes off. She could slay men with a single look but never had to resort to cheap or demeaning tactics. Barbara Stanwyck was also an intriguing mixture of both masculine and feminine traits: a strong, charismatic, sexy woman. I soon realized that beauty had little to do with what was on the surface but that it ultimately derived from self-confidence, intelligence, pride in being a woman, understated elegance and the ability to select at will the appropriate weapon from one's feminine arsenal and employ it to devastating effect. Part of the self-confidence, I realized, had to come from knowing that you looked good, but that was not the same as being pretty.

I realized too that I had to feed my mind as carefully and selectively as I was feeding my body if I wanted to grow and blossom in the right direction. I read anything and everything I could get my hands on that I deemed appropriate. I remembered that the first book I had read in English at Ladbroke Upper School had been the biography of Mao Tse-tung, followed by Karl Marx's *Communist Manifesto*. Not because I had any deeply felt political views but because I wanted to improve my knowledge of history and politics. Then, as ever, I continued to read avidly and set about reading *The Book of the Courtier* by the Renaissance Italian writer Baldassare Castiglione, who died in Toledo in 1529 and whose portrait by Raphael is in the Louvre.

Castiglione's masterpiece deals with the philosophies of taste, love, protocol and etiquette and was read throughout Europe for many centuries as the definitive book on manners. The writer seemed to be so full of advice which I could use. He counselled, for instance, that friendships must be carefully made and chosen. He warned that the more information you give others about yourself, the more you belong to them and the harder it is to part company with them, so that you become a hostage of sorts. He talked about love, saying that when only two people knew about their *affaire de coeur* it was exciting but that as soon as one more person shared their secret the excitement was diminished, and the more people who learnt of the liaison the more the pleasure was diluted. Secrecy, he said, made love intense and important. To keep a man interested and intrigued, he suggested, a woman should be different and never predictable. She must change continually.

I read Machiavelli's *The Prince* and *Discourses* and the novels of Balzac. I read about history, medicine, science, technology and banking – in fact, anything that I could persuade people to tell me about. I read the biographies of famous figures such as Henry Kissinger in an attempt to understand the psychology of powerful men, and novels such as Oscar Wilde's *The Picture of Dorian Gray*, which made me think about the essence of youth and further inspired me to approach life with determination and to give no quarter. Sitting in the library at work, I used to force myself to memorize paragraphs from books, the names and dates of famous people, thereby sharpening my brain power and broadening my knowledge. I figured that as knowledge was power, a good, quick and versatile brain would mean that I could use my knowledge very productively. I spent as much time as I could with intelligent people and whenever they talked about a topic or book or recommended something to me, I would set out to discover as much about it as possible.

In addition, I devoured books by less high-brow writers such as Sidney Sheldon for light reading and for the glimpses they gave me into the superficial worlds of the rich, powerful and romantic. I particularly recall the heroine in Sheldon's book *The Other Side of Midnight*, who , despite being badly hurt emotionally and not being outstandingly beautiful, managed to conquer the heart of the richest man in the world with her feminine prowess. It was her confidence and her femininity that made everyone fall in love with her. The majority of readers regard these books as pure escapism and are content to remain in their role as small players in life's rich pageant, merely dreaming of other, more exciting worlds. But I wanted to learn from them so that when the time came I would know how to deport myself in the environment these books depicted. Glossy magazines were another source of information on the world of which I wanted to become an active part, full of information about clothes, make-up, sex, travel, food, drink, hotels and interior decoration.

It must seem rather unclear how, over that pivotal period of less than eighteen months, I went from being an anorexic eighteen-year-old suffering from depression and with no sexual experience of any kind to what must appear, to all intents and purposes, to be a scheming, mercenary and ruthless woman. There were several factors at play, all of which contributed to this apparently dramatic and speedy metamorphosis. First of all I was absolutely desperate to get away from my mother, whom I had grown to hate because of her continued malice, harassment and emotional cruelty. I could not face the prospect of living with her much longer and I knew that it would be an inordinately long time before I would be able to get a home of my own on the salary I was then earning. I didn't want to go through the process of flat-sharing as a temporary state of affairs. Besides, through the kindness and benevolence of Lady Bird, as well as through my own powers of observation, I had perceived, albeit briefly, a lifestyle which I felt, after my years of suffering, was due to me on merit.

I had proved an enormous amount to myself by learning English, passing all my exams and making a good start to my professional life through hard work, application and diligence. It was my opinion that with my self-confidence remarkably still intact, and my driving ambition and determination, I could easily combine all my assets so as to advance by means that seemed to me to be entirely justified, logical and straight-forward. As for my materialistic attitude towards men surfacing at such a young age, I can only say that I had never encountered any men to make me think otherwise. Perhaps if I had been lucky enough to have enjoyed all the benefits of a normal family life and received more confidence-building support and approval from those around me, then my seemingly calculating and frosty disposition towards the opposite gender might have been different. But I didn't and I make no apologies for the attitude which I was to so successfully adopt for the next seventeen years. Some may view this as a type of protracted revenge for the disappointments of my childhood and if that is the case then so be it.

My attraction to older, powerful men was not, as some would have one believe, a wicked perversion. It was a deliberately structured convenience which I used as a platform to independence, influence and status. As a rule, I didn't like men – I never had – and ever since the awareness of my own sexuality and persuasive ability I have regarded them, with a few exceptions, as fair game for whatever purpose I saw fit. I have used their misplaced sense of ego, their pathetic need for sexual conquest, their conveniently flexible ideas of ethics and their warped moralities extremely effectively for my own advancement.

By now I was getting ready to leave the London School of Hygiene and Tropical Medicine as I had developed a very strong and compelling vision of where I wanted to direct my life.

4

The Learning Process

Strange to relate, but having made the decision to change so drastically the course of my life, I developed a certain peace of mind which enabled me to think in a very lucid and practical manner.

I thought continually about ways in which I could improve myself and thus my situation. I was still obliged to live with my mother but at least I was able to earn money myself and now had a track record of employment, albeit a short one. The next priority seemed to be to discover a way of escaping from all those things which were making me unhappy. This meant finding a way to afford a place of my own while at the same time taking as many courses as I could which would ultimately help me to acquire the knowledge I felt I needed to become the person I had now set out to become. Although I had enjoyed working at the School of Hygiene and Tropical Medicine and the people there had been very kind to me, I knew that I had to look for a position that was more likely to bring me into contact with a mentor.

One of the benefits about working at the School had been the opportunities which it had given me to learn about medicine and medical research. It had certainly been interesting and had broadened my knowledge a good deal. But I now needed to be somewhere where I could learn more about business and the world of commerce. I had read enough to know that all the great wealth in the world is created in the first place by people who buy and sell goods and products as well as offer essential services and finance great projects. Anyone who makes deals with governments is going to be moving among people of real power and influence who themselves possess great wealth. From what I could tell, there are fortunes to be made in virtually every line of business as long as there is a steady rate of supply and demand, but it is those who are involved with the supply of essentials, luxury items and technology of all sorts who grow to be the richest and wield the most influence in the world.

Initially I spent a few months working in the data-processing department of Mercedes-Benz UK. There I made some very useful contacts and, for no reason other than I was very well presented, confident, outgoing and ambitious, I came to the attention of some of the very top figures in the company. There were two reasons why I decided not to stay there too long. The first was that where I worked was on the Great Western Road on the way to Heathrow Airport. It was awkward and time-consuming to get there and back and when I worked overtime at weekends I actually found myself out of pocket with regard to travelling expenses. The second reason was that my prospects for upward mobility were limited, as was the likelihood of my encountering the type of people who would open doors of opportunity for me.

My next move was to a company of consulting engineers by the name of Sir William Halcrow & Partners. I worked in a good position in their computer department and immediately felt comfortable in the atmosphere of a company handling multimillion-pound engineering contracts all over the world. There was an almost palpable air of success and prosperity about the offices at Newcombe House, Notting Hill Gate. The people here were dealing at the very highest levels with governments and major industrial corporations. Here the worlds of construction, finance and technology seemed to merge and a constant stream of highly important people flowed in and out of the offices. There were numerous meetings with government representatives, financiers, architects and designers as well as the heads of major corporations, industrialists and figures from the international petrochemical industry. It was a very exciting company for which to work and offered considerable opportunities, having offices all over the world.

I felt that I was now in the right place to move forward, but that didn't mean that I could sit back and wait for something to happen. There were, as now, hundreds of thousands of bright young women working in corporations and businesses all over the world. No one was going to notice me just because I was doing a good job working at a keyboard in the computer department. I had to continue to seek out the individuals from whom I could learn how to create the most impressive self-image so that I could rise above the crowd.

One of the ways which I had learnt was to make the most of one's looks. I have never regarded myself as beautiful in the classic sense, although I am fortunately possessed of some fine features and am able to make the most of my facial assets. I have always loved and been fascinated by make-up, right from when I was very little. I distinctly remember attending my first communion at the age of eight. This was while my grandmother was still alive and it was decided to take advantage of one of my mother's rare visits to Valencia. The ceremony in the Church of San Francisco de Borja was a solemn, dignified and important event for a little girl and I was very excited. Actually I hated the dress, which I was forced to wear by my mother, and I remember wanting to wear something completely different.

The best part, however, was that I was allowed to wear a little make-up and paint my small nails. Apart from that occasion I had been forbidden by my mother to play with make-up, which I didn't really know how to apply anyway, and as a child it became a naughty girl's game which I indulged in very infrequently and only when I knew it to be very safe. Aunt Francisca was the first person who really opened my eyes to the possibilities of make-up, first on her visits back to Valencia and later when I was with her in London, where she worked as a housekeeper for a wealthy Greek family. She was a very beautiful woman, always immaculately dressed, and used to wear wigs in order to alter her appearance, which was also regarded as very fashionable at the time. She was the person who introduced me to the Mary Quant range, which was very popular in the seventies. I used to be fascinated by her eyeliners and Quant, along with a number of other cosmetic companies in that era, was producing and promoting metallic eye shadows and 'glitter' make-up, which everyone was using. That, however, was the point. If 'everyone' was now able to buy the same products over the counter, and could learn how to use them from magazines, I was going to have to go further, digging deeper into the secrets and mysteries of *maquillage* if I was to be noticed above other women.

Later on I was so determined to become 'the perfect woman' that I took a course at the Lucie Clayton School of Modelling in Knightsbridge.

I also bought a number of books on make-up for professionals in the theatre and film industries, and visited Carita in Paris for special make-ups, in order to learn each step of the beautifying process for myself. I have always regarded my eyes as one of my strongest features ('greenfinch' eyes as they were described by Carol Sarler in the *Sunday Times Magazine*), so I learnt how to apply mascara on my dark-blonde lashes to enhance them without making them look unnatural and how to pluck and shape my eyebrows from below so as not to end up resembling a clown. I also developed my own way of doing my eye make-up using Chinese calligraphy brushes. I learnt that it is important to enhance only one feature on a face, either the eyes or the lips – never both, because that can look overpowering and unnatural. If you pay a lot of attention to your eyes, then you should use only pale colours on the lips to finish off the look in a subtle way. I became a great believer in little tricks like matching nail varnish to lipstick so that they can blend with the clothes that you have selected.

These little touches made an enormous difference to the way I looked compared with others, even though my wardrobe at the time was still quite limited. I could see that very few women took the trouble to put the finishing touches to their appearances except on very special occasions such as weddings. They seemed not to be bothered about the impression they made on the people around them on a day-to-day basis and to have developed certain make-up habits probably learnt from their equally inept mothers, and then stuck to them without thinking how to develop or adapt them to suit changing fashions and different situations. In short, they seemed not to be putting any thought into the way they looked and I concluded that this gave out the message that they didn't want to be noticed and consequently didn't want to be successful. It was my intention from the very beginning of my newly developed philosophy that I intended to send out very different and clear messages and make sure that these were noticed.

However much professional advice you take about your appearance, a good deal is still a matter of trial and error, personal taste and common sense. Many people simply do not have the sense of order and balance needed to put their overall look together. I do believe, however, that if you are exposed from a young age to things such as good-quality magazines and films you can learn simply by absorbing what is around you. It is a sort of unconscious osmosis, although I suspect that there has to be an inherent desire to learn as well as a need to be open-minded. The chances are that someone who has been brought up in an ugly and colourless environment and who has no intuitive wish to develop a feel for the aesthetic will find that they do not have the scope for nurturing a sense of beauty.

One of the difficulties for any woman determined to be beautiful is to know where to draw the line, when to accept the laws of nature and let artifice go no further. Over the years I have developed some strong views about cosmetic surgery. I think that if someone is deeply unhappy with the shape of their nose or if their ears protrude too much, then, for the sake of their self-confidence, it may be well worth their while to undergo surgery to make the necessary changes. On the other hand, I admire and respect those who are able to overcome and remain unaffected by a less than attractive facial feature and who compensate by having outgoing and confident personalities. With regard to face-lifts, I can only say that there is a great deal of dignity in growing old naturally and with calm resignation. A positive attitude and a lot of self-confidence and enthusiasm will keep the mind and the faculties eternally youthful long after the body has accepted the inevitability of age. Apart from having one tooth straightened, I have been very lucky in never having felt the need to improve on the face nature has bestowed on me.

As a little girl, one of my best physical assets was my long, soft hair, even though when I came to England I had it all cut off in a desire to have a page-boy cut, which was very fashionable at the time. In my twenties I began to curl it in order to achieve a more glamorous look. In one respect I have been very lucky: I have always been taken for much younger than my age. But at that stage, with my eyes firmly focused on material and financial ambitions, I wanted to be taken seriously. Nonetheless, I decided to put highlights into my hair, which I have kept partly because it suits my pale skin but also as I had to pander a little to the whims of those whom I intended to use as rungs on the ladder to independence. In time I was able to afford good hairdressers and the very best make-up just as I was able to acquire good clothes and achieve precisely the look I wanted. But lack of money is never a valid excuse for any woman not to learn how to be beautiful and look after herself. Anyone can get access to films and magazines and watch how other people achieve glamour and feminine appeal, and the shops are full of wonderful and relatively inexpensive beauty products with which to experiment.

Having unusually pale skin, I never developed a taste for sunbathing even when it was considered very fashionable to be as brown as possible. I never particularly enjoyed going to beaches, which I found boring, or liked the look of fair-haired women with deeply tanned skins that will eventually ensure that they end up looking like old discarded saddle-bags. I preferred to spend my time indoors developing the 'pale and interesting' look and anyway I was far too busy to devote hours to cooking myself in the sun when I could not envisage any good reason for doing so. My skin always burnt quickly and was just not suited to sunbathing. Because we now know that a good many forms of skin cancer can develop through excessive absorption of the sun's ultraviolet rays, I would advise all women to avoid lengthy exposure to the sun whenever possible.

The way a woman carries herself is also a crucial aspect of her persona and for creating an aura of femininity. I studied most carefully the way elegant women, including film stars and models, walked and sat down, then taught myself to do the same. I realized that most women make the mistake of not walking tall enough, of not moving in a graceful and fluid way. They also wear clothes that don't suit them, thereby making it quite plain that they are trying to achieve a look on the outside that they do not feel within themselves. If a woman has confidence in her appearance, she can get away with wearing almost anything as long as it is of good quality.

Improving the way I looked was only part of the struggle. I also needed to improve the way I sounded. Despite having mastered the English language, I wanted to be able to make conversation in an intelligent and educated way, which meant that I needed the vocabulary and phrasing of someone for whom English was their native tongue. I spent many hours watching political debates and educational programmes on television and later on even went to the trouble of taking elocution lessons. The lady whose help I sought was Professor Daphne de Campanet, a delicate and incredibly erudite woman. She was wonderfully helpful and I spent nearly eighteen months with her learning to project my voice, improve my pronunciation and speak more clearly. It was her view that I ought not to lose my Spanish accent because it was part of my personality, but she taught me to slow down my speech patterns and not to sound as if I was always running out of time. She helped me with my reading, introducing me to the great English classics, poetry, the plays of Shakespeare and the tales of Chaucer, to develop my understanding of the roots of the language.

I was working all the time to build and exercise my mind but I had never been a great fan of physical exercise. Although I now belong to one of the best health clubs in London, the Peak at the Hyatt Carlton in Cadogan Square and before that at the Meridien in Piccadilly, I find the demands of disciplined exercise unnatural and an imposition. Everyone is different, but I think that exercise should fit into your way of life and that if one has a good diet then things like walking and climbing stairs rather than taking the lift are usually enough to ensure that the body stays fit. They also have the advantage of being free.

Many people make the mistake of thinking that all you need to be successful is a little luck, and they constantly bemoan their lack of progress and promotion, blaming it on the lack of good fortune. A little luck now and then is certainly very welcome but it is never enough on its own. If one lacks the intelligence to know what to do when the breaks come, then they might as well not have come at all. The only true path to success is determination, hard work and a clear vision of what you want to achieve with your life.

Shortly after I arrived at Halcrow's a friend called Alicia, who was an engineer with the company, told me that she was moving back to Venezuela with her husband, as she was expecting a baby, and invited me to her farewell party. This was to be rather a formative moment in my life and one that I very nearly forsook. It had been my intention to take a brief holiday in Spain and, despite my determined intentions to make something of my life no matter what the cost, I still had a strong degree of compassion and kindness within me. Therefore I had planned to go back to Gijón to visit Mercedes, Ramón and their family, thinking that they might have changed in the intervening two years since I had last seen them. I was on my way back from the bank, where I had collected some Spanish currency, when I remembered my friend's leaving party upstairs at a local pub.

There Alicia introduced me to Noel Cochrane, who, she said, had been her guide and mentor during her time in England and a man who was soon to become the company's senior partner. 'He is one of the greatest men I have ever met,' she explained as she took me over to meet him. Later on I discovered that Noel was a truly kind and philanthropic man with the most honourable and correct intentions, he often took on protégés, especially young people whom he brought to England from universities in South America to give them engineering experience, training them up and then sending them back to work in Halcrow's office in Quito, Colombia. Noel and his wife were always very hospitable and kind to these students while they were in England, making sure that their extended visits were comfortable and helping them to gain any qualifications or work experience they might need.

Noel was a man who would change and reshape my life completely over the next few years. He was then in his late fifties, grey-haired, a softly spoken, gentle and sensitive man. I immediately felt very comfortable with him as we talked. When the time eventually came for me to go back to the office, we left together.

'I just have to collect something from my car,' he said. 'Would you mind taking a little detour?'

I was quite content to spend a little more time talking to him as we walked along and expressed no outward reaction when he led me to a car which I had long been admiring from my office window: a dark-blue Ferrari. As one of my new disciplines I had trained myself never to react openly or with surprise to anything I encountered but simply to behave as if unimpressed and familiar with the grandoise and luxurious.

'I couldn't imagine a man like you driving a car like this,' I remarked.

'What do you mean?' he asked, turning around. 'Am I too old?'

'No of course not,' I laughed. 'I just thought someone more . . .' – I searched desperately for the right word – '. . . playful would be driving it.'

The 'think before you speak' lesson was immediately learnt and never forgotten. I was still going through the learning process.

We became close friends from then on, although we didn't start to have an affair for another year or so. In the words of the French novelist Emile Zola, Noel became 'my first serious protector'. I confess that I very much wanted him to be my first lover from the beginning but he said that at eighteen I was too young. The reason that I wanted him so badly was that in my naïvety I believed that were I go to bed with him I would have succeeded in my goal of ensnaring and capturing the heart of a man despite the fact that after only a short time I had him eating out of the palm of my hand. Only later in my life did I learn that going to bed with a man could actually be little other than a mere physical act, devoid of emotion, and that the capture of a man's heart and spirit was an emotional and not a physical conquest. At eighteen I had had little sexual experience at all other than a few tentative and insignificant acts and was still technically a virgin. I had had a short but close relationship with a handsome work colleague who was in his mid to late twenties. He was of Indian and Scandinavian extraction and came from a wealthy and affluent family. I remember that he had a very attractive combination of dark skin, fair hair and blue eyes and I enjoyed spending time with him and his family even though I never fell in love with him. In fact, I can confidently say that I didn't truly fall in love until much later in my life and ended up quite happily marrying the man. As for my other liaisons, I admit that occasionally I cared for and even became fond of a few men, but it was a rarity and something that for me only complicated matters.

I was understandably curious about sex and interested in much the same way that I was interested in learning about business, literature, fashion, etiquette, deportment, beauty and all the other numerous subjects encompassed by my philosophy of becoming the complete and perfect woman. I wanted to have sexual experience inasmuch as it would become another of those 'weapons' in my arsenal of femininity, but I didn't want it to be with just anyone – only with the best. I wanted an older man who could teach me all I needed to know for the future so that I could invest in myself. He would be a man who was important and of significance, who had the chance to choose from many women but actively chose to be with me because he considered me someone special. It was my intention to learn from the best teacher I could find, which meant men of experience, conversant with giving pleasure to a woman, rather than men of youth and beauty, whom I associate with clumsiness and ineptitude.

In general I have found that older men are not as interested in the physical, sexual act as society seems to believe. Many of them simply enjoy the visual and sensual attractions of a woman. There are some who have more unusual interests of a more fetishistic and self-humiliating nature. But that rarely has anything to do with lovemaking and it is hard for a woman to respect this type of man even though she may be prepared, because this activity is normally only a small part of a close relationship, to indulge him in return for all the other aspects of a warm and fruitful liaison.

As should be the case with all women, I have never been shy of exploring my sexuality. There are, of course, certain acts which I know instinctively I would not enjoy, although on occasion I have been tempted by sheer curiosity to experiment but ultimately found that I derived little or no pleasure. Most adults, unless seriously sexually repressed, are inherently aware of their sexual preferences and should be allowed to pursue them freely without interference unless, of course, they infringe the law or public decency. I am a very open-minded person and nothing could really surprise me any more about human sexuality. When it took my fancy or suited me, I have indulged in most 'bedroom games', but I like to pride myself that it was always with style, elegance and finesse. However, most of the men in my life have been more interested in me as a companion, an intelligent and beautiful woman on their arm and someone who is outwardly caring and interested in their lives. When this is the case the sexual act plays only a small part in a loving relationship.

I have also always been of the belief that true lovemaking can only happen between partners who genuinely care deeply for each other and when the physical act of love becomes an extension of the genuine feelings they have for one another. Anything other than that is no more than an act of which any one of God's creatures is capable. Lovemaking is an emotional activity and not to be confused with anything else.

There is, however, a whole world which is more important than the sexual one, and that is the exciting and pleasurable field of sensuality. The sexual act should represent one small aspect in a physical relationship, the bed itself merely an accoutrement in an armoury of pleasures. Physical skills such as the ability to massage are very important. Most successful men work hard and are often exhausted by the time they come to unwind with their chosen partners. They want to be able to relax, to let go of the self-control and dynamism they have been employing all day and give themselves over to someone they love, trust and desire. Consequently they may derive as much pleasure from watching a beautiful woman dress or undress or take a bath, and from being given a gentle and soothing massage, as from the relief normally associated with the sexual act. Having discovered that one of my own greatest indulgences is to receive a thorough and professional massage, I have come to learn about the things that work, that cause one to relax or make one comfortable, and these techniques I have adapted for use on the men I have known. The feet, for example, are very sensitive to the touch, and the art and benefits of reflexology are greatly underestimated, as is a gentle scalp massage. To feel one's partner's fingers working on your skin, massaging your body, penetrating down to the muscles and tendons, is a glorious release from stress and tension. There is no law that says a massage must ultimately lead to sex. It all depends on one's mood at the time: to many people, bathing in the warm glow after a massage is sometimes sufficient without having to go further.

I have always been very interested in the mental games of sex, being willing and able to realize the fantasies that men have and then making them work to achieve these dreams. In order to keep a man keen and interested, it is never good to allow him to believe that he will always get what he wants otherwise he will rush straight in and the whole adventure will be over before either party has a chance to savour and enjoy the benefits. Everything a woman does should be designed to make the man on whom she has designs desire her more. In *Nana*, Zola described a scene where the Comte Muffat is watching Nana dressing to go on stage. The Comte, according to Zola, is 'filled with a frantic longing for the young woman's painted charms'. Later Zola tells how the Comte 'would have abjured everything, sold everything to possess her for a single hour that very night. His youth, the lustful puberty of adolescence, was awakening within him at last, flaring up suddenly in the frigidity of the Catholic and the dignity of the middle-aged man.' By seducing him visually, Nana completely captures the Comte's heart, until eventually he is willing to offer her anything. 'I'd make your every wish come true,' he declares, 'to have you all to myself. I'd give my whole fortune . . . and if you agreed to be mine alone, why, then I'd want you to be the loveliest, richest woman on earth, with carriages, and diamonds and dresses.'

That, in my view, is the correct way to seduce a man and make him fall in love with you and if genealogical history is to be believed then an impressive percentage of titled families in the upper echelons of most of English and European society can boast of the success of such clever and devious methods from showgirls, dancers and 'good-time girls' down the ages. Nowadays it seems that women are prepared to sacrifice themselves for a dinner or small gift, thereby betraying the low level of their own self-worth when, with a little more courage and higher personal esteem, their virtue could command a higher price than a meal or a bunch of flowers.

Within the confines of a relationship, it is important to make a man feel comfortable enough to talk about his fantasies, which, if not too out-rageous or impossible, his partner can put into practice should she be willing. He must never be made to feel that what he desires is offensive, laughable or ridiculous, otherwise he will be intimidated and possibly too embarrassed to continue the relationship. There are a few standard and frequently encountered fantasies that men have but sadly most wives or girlfriends don't know that their partners harbour these secret desires. If a woman wishes to become a great lover she should be willing to at least discuss these things without embarrassment. Depending on the regard in which she holds the man of the moment, she may or may not choose to indulge him. Above anything else a lover must try to be accommodating, and as long as both parties agree, there is no reason why either should ever develop feelings of jealousy or discomfort. Open relationships are not for everyone, however, and without doubt most people are happy with the feelings of security engendered by knowing that their partner is loyal and not involved with other lovers.

While a woman should endeavour to find out as much as she can about a man's ambitions and desires, she must, at the same time, not give away too many of her own secrets in the process. A woman's power lies in keeping her knowledge to herself. Later, when the time is right and she has encountered a special man or else wants to accomplish a certain aim, she might also be willing to trust her partner with a few secrets of her own. The sharing of such things in a close relationship and the demonstration of mutual trust can produce a long-lasting bond. In my experience, it is not hard to get a man to talk about himself, nor is it too difficult to deflect him from showing too much interest in you.

Virtually all women know how to get a man they desire into bed, but very few know how to win his heart and mind and keep him there. To do that you must first find out all his needs and then, when possible, satisfy them gradually. Knowing that you have the power to do this can be immensely satisfying and in my case I regarded it as a considerable achievement. When you select someone whom you want to fall in love with you, you can appear on the surface to be giving yourself willingly and unconditionally but actually be calculating and controlling every move that you make with him being totally unaware of it.

I was convinced, having developed my own personal philosophy, that the mind had to be the driving force for a successful woman – not just the body. Any woman who relied exclusively on her physical and sexual attributes in order to progress, I concluded, was doomed to failure and was inevitably going to be used and then discarded by the men to whom she gave herself, unable to win either their respect or loyalty. I had no intention of allowing that to happen to me and it was always my intention to find a perfect balance and combination of the two. In return for these gifts of the sensual, sexual and emotional rewards, I expected the men in my life to provide me with the freedom and support to do as I pleased. My aim was to manoeuvre myself into a position where I could explore their emotional and physical needs as well as their desires and discover what it was precisely that they sought from being with me. I would then allow them to have what they wanted, in small measures, and only at a time when it suited me to give it to them. Of course, at the age of nineteen with my ambitions now clearly defined, I was impatient to start on my exploration of the male psyche, but Noel forced me to bide my time. His reluctance to take advantage of my youthfulness and zeal was frustrating but ultimately made me respect him all the more.

I was certainly a little frustrated by this delay but also relieved to find a man who was willing to treat me with respect and consideration and cared about my welfare. I knew that I didn't want to be with a man who was pouncing on me every moment of the day and night. I wanted to be with men who were willing to give me a lot of time to myself. Powerful and successful men are always busy with other aspects of their lives, which means that their women are free to indulge themselves for a large proportion of the day. The men are intent on ensuring that their women are cared for and given whatever they need during those idle hours, and in order to be certain of that they provide the necessary financial support. This is an entirely different concept from the practice of paying for sex. In that circumstance the man simply pays a fee for services rendered. It might seem a generous rate compared with the sort of money which a woman can earn doing an average job, but it is nowhere near enough to keep them in true luxury and allow them to build up serious capital. By renting out their bodies rather than their abilities and brains, they are in no position to expect introductions and to make social and business contracts through the men that they take to bed and so are not able to truly gain control of their destinies. They cannot expect to have long-term strategies and in many cases are unable to make enough cash to allow them to look ahead for more than a few weeks. There is no security, no prospect of advancement and little chance of serious emotional and financial success.

Most people want to find one special person and spend their whole lives together happily raising a family. While I would sometimes entertain the fantasy of meeting one man who so completely fulfilled all my dreams that I would need no other, my experience of family life had been such a nightmare that I knew, in the clear light of day, that this was never likely to materialize. My cynicism was based on the travesties of marriage I had seen in Spain and elsewhere and I knew for certain that I wanted something very different from those squalid and depressing relationships. Perhaps sadly, I was never able to confide my plans to anyone. Not because I didn't have any friends but because even I knew that my views, values and priorities were not likely to encounter tolerance and understanding from many people. I also felt that were I to share my ambitions I might in some way jeopardize their coming to fruition, make myself a hostage to others and somehow dissipate my power. I intended to keep my plans to myself and carefully nurture and fine-tune them away from the likelihood of others' outrage, mockery and disapproval.

Once he had taken me under his wing, Noel opened up his whole life to me. He took me to his family home in the country at weekends and Christmas and listened patiently when I talked about my unhappy relationship with my mother and the difficulties of my childhood. I found that I was able to confide everything about my anguish and frustration to him while still keeping in mind my carefully thought out personal philosophy and never losing sight of my future needs. He was very kind to me, gently advising me but never condemning my mother for the way she behaved toward me. Although my mother knew that I had become his protégé and that I was spending time with him and his family while still working at Halcrow's, she was never aware of the true nature of our relationship.

There was an incident that occurred approximately three months or so after Noel and I had first met but after we had become quite close. I inadvertently came across some letters and poems which he had written to his secretary some years previously, and Noel confided to me that he had been in love with her. Despite the fact that she had not returned his sentiments and indeed even rebuffed him quite firmly, I could not help but be rather shocked by this revelation. Not because being infatuated with one woman while being married to another came as any surprise to me, but because the woman was so incredibly plain, dumpy and unattractive. I will confess that from that moment on, my attitude towards Noel altered considerably as I now began to question his standards. The whole business was a disappointment to me, but it succeeded in strengthening my personal resolve to persevere with my ambitions and make full use of Noel's status, connections and affluence.

Outwardly I showed no reaction to this occurrence and our relationship continued. Over the next year and a half I continued working in the computer department, with a brief stint as a translator for the foreign desk. Over time I virtually became a member of Noel's family, going down to the house in the country at weekends and sitting round the table with their children, who were all older than me and all of whom I later saw marry and have children of their own. The whole family were very relaxed with me, quite used to their father bringing home young protégées who were essentially being groomed for glittering careers in the company. Noel's wife, Christine Cochrane, was a tall, slim, quiet woman who had trained as a psychotherapist and was quite content living in the country during the week while her husband made use of the company penthouse near the office in Notting Hill. Noel told me that he and Christine led their own separate lives in many respects, which didn't really concern me much except that it made me think he perhaps wanted to justify our growing relationship as much to me as to himself.

Noel and I finally became lovers a year after that initial meeting at Alicia's farewell party. I say lovers, but in all honesty there was little actual sexual activity and whatever transpired was of a fairly tame nature. Technically I was to remain a virgin for a little while longer. However, we would meet once a week during the day at the company's penthouse, where Noel, because he was now the senior partner, lived while in London. At weekends either I went and stayed with his family down in the country, where everything was correct and proper, or he would take me for lunch in country hotels and stately homes. We both loved driving around the countryside in the Ferrari, exploring and looking for new places. Usually I was happy to let him choose where we would go, but if I read of an interesting restaurant or hotel I might ask to go there and he would always agree to take me. Noel was a kind and honourable man who treated me beautifully and with great respect. He did finally fall in love with me and we were to remain close. Later he even gave me away at my wedding to my first husband. Through Noel I began to meet other interesting people and made some useful contacts, as had always been my ambition, while at the same time building my own social life via work colleagues.

Throughout my time at Halcrow's I continued to live with my mother in Lansdowne Walk. I engineered things in such a way that after two years with the firm I finally convinced Noel and Christine that I could no longer bear living with my mother, because of the distress it was causing me, and with some further gentle persuasion on my part the Cochranes offered first of all to rent and a few months later to buy me a studio apartment in St John's Wood. Initially the money was an interest-free loan and I remember that the cheque with which the flat was purchased was drawn on their joint account.

Shortly after I acquired the apartment Noel and I decided that I should leave Halcrow's and start to attend courses that would increase my chances of embarking on a successful, professional business career. I recall being extremely pleased with myself for having achieved a number of goals so quickly. Although not yet financially independent, I had a mentor who was prepared to look after me, a delightful studio flat in a smart area of London and the prospect of doing whatever courses I wanted in order to further my career and realize my ambitions.

Before attending any courses, however, I still wanted to work and earn some money for myself as well as increase my business contacts. So I found myself an extremely worthwhile job at the Arab League, a non-political organization in Green Street, Mayfair. There I stayed for three months in the press office, my work involving searching for all information appearing in the English press about the Arab world and filing it away in the library. Glamorous, no. But ultimately useful beyond belief. Once a month I would help organize high-level meetings with all the Arab ambassadors in London to discuss the Middle East situation. Although I was not present at these meetings, it gave me the opportunity to encounter in a professional capacity many important Middle Eastern figures whose influence and position I was to use later on. It also gave me access to a considerable volume of useful information and was the perfect opportunity for me to gain more knowledge about an important geopolitical and economic part of the world. Moreover, it would assist me when talking to people I met socially, and indeed I found that I had a good rapport with a good number of the Arabs that I encountered and they appreciated my understanding of their culture. This experience was to prove very important later in my life.

It was during my brief stint at the Arab League that I met the man to whom I technically surrendered my virginity. He was a kind, gentle man in his late forties who was the personal and private physician to the Ruler of Qatar, one of the Arab Emirates. I was introduced to him at an official function to which I had been invited by a mutual friend and despite all the stories that one reads about the supposedly deep emotional impression left on a woman by the first man with whom she sleeps, the experience was not particularly memorable, did not result in any form of emotional or other attachment and, as far as I was concerned, was no more than a physical technicality.

Noel was encouraging me all the time to do whatever I felt was going to prove useful for the career he and I were planning for me. Although I didn't enrol in any courses immediately, it was my firm intention to do so in order to fill in whatever gaps I felt there might be in my professional abilities. I worked as a translator for another firm of consulting engineers but this was short-lived as there developed some interesting changes in my status and accommodation.

I had been living in the studio flat in St John's Wood for only a year or so when the opportunity arose for me to move to a bigger place. Noel had completed his term as senior partner at Halcrow's and although he was still with the firm in a very elevated capacity he no longer had the use of the penthouse flat near the office. He had therefore bought himself an apartment in a smart and luxurious building in Fulham called Alder Lodge, which overlooked the river on one side and a courtyard and central fountain on the other. The facilities were superb and included a swimming pool and sauna. Soon after he bought the flat an opportunity arose to acquire another apartment in the same building. Noel liked the idea of my being very near to him and it did not take much persuasion to get him to buy the flat for me. It was purchased with the proceeds of the sale of the St John's Wood flat and quite a bit more on top. It was a beautiful apartment, a good deal larger than what I had been used to and I wanted to turn it into something very special and luxurious. It had two bedrooms and two bathrooms, a magnificent drawing-room, a dining-room and a kitchen. As with my studio flat, I selected the furniture, wallpaper and fabrics and decorated the whole place myself. I went to Zarachs in South Audley Street for the Parisian wallpaper and to Turri of Milan for the furniture, as well as acquiring all the latest technical gadgets for the kitchen. A neighbour later fell in love with the apartment after I had finished it and bought it from me two years later at a huge profit.

During this time I was still occasionally going down to the country with Noel to see his wife and children, who genuinely considered me a member of the family. Christine was unaware that I had left the studio and was now living in Fulham, but she knew that I was no longer at Halcrow's. How Noel managed to explain our continuing relationship to his wife I shall never know, but I remember thinking that even though she looked upon me as a daughter it must have seemed a little strange the two of us turning up together, Noel a man of over sixty and me a beautiful and glamorous girl of twenty-one. However, it has always seemed to me that women are capable of justifying all kinds of things to themselves when they don't want to face the possible consequences of accepting reality. Gradually the number of my visits to the country diminished and then they ceased altogether when, by chance, Christine came across a credit-card receipt and invoice for a case of champagne that Noel had been kind enough to send to me for Christmas that year. On the invoice was not only Noel's address at Alder Lodge but the address to which the champagne had been sent. This bore my name but a different flat number in the same building. Christine then realized what was going on and, according to Noel, began to play the role of the aggrieved, betrayed and deeply offended wife after he had confessed to her that he was in love with me.

Over the years I have heard almost every excuse under the sun as to why women stay with their husbands despite their partner's repeated infidelity with every woman they can seduce. The reasons that men state for staying with wives to whom they are no longer attracted or for whom they care very little are also fairly diverse and equally pathetic. The wives are usually too frightened and insecure and lack the independent means to leave these deceitful men and prefer instead to turn a blind eye to their husband's little peccadilloes rather than have the courage to condemn them and walk out. 'If you weren't such fools,' Nana tells Comte Muffat in Zola's novel, 'you'd be as nice to your wives as you are to us, and if your wives weren't idiots they'll take as much trouble to keep you as we do to catch you . . . instead of behaving as they do.'

Within a year of all this happening, I had yet another fortunate encounter which was to greatly assist me in further developing my personal plan for wealth, independence and financial security. In late 1978 I met Joseph Tadros at the Grosvenor House Hotel in Park Lane. He was Greek by nationality and he lived and worked in the Sudan. I was at the hotel in order to have tea with a Spanish friend of mind called Rosa. She had not turned up within an hour of our appointed rendezvous and, highly irritated at being let down, I decided to go home. As I emerged into Park Lane my bad temper was made even worse by the fact that rain was now bouncing off the pavement and all the taxis in Mayfair seemed to have disappeared in the cloudburst. Joseph appeared out of the downpour like a guardian angel and offered to help me find a cab. We got talking and after a few minutes he managed to calm me down and invited me back into the hotel for a glass of champagne. He told me that he was an engineer involved in government business in the Sudan and a shareholder in the Sudanese national airline. Tall, slim and grey-haired, Joseph was a well-mannered man in his late forties. He was unmarried and had a sister in London who was a scientist. I felt comfortable with him and able to talk to him as an equal because of my experiences at Halcrow's. Before long I was actually beginning to feel grateful to Rosa for proving so unreliable.

After our drink Joseph told me he was planning to walk the short distance to Farm Street Church if the rain let up.

'That is the church I sometimes go to for Sunday Mass,' I told him and he invited me to join him. Outside the pavements were still glistening but the skies were now clear and the air felt fresh as we walked and continued our conversation. Joseph invited me to dinner that evening to a restaurant ship moored on the Thames near the Houses of Parliament which was very popular at the time and called the *Hispaniola*.

In all, our relationship was to last a total of twelve years, during which Joseph was extremely kind to me. He was, in fact, the first man to ask me to marry him and I was the first woman with whom he had ever wanted to start a family. My answer then was that one day I would seriously consider his flattering proposal. However, I didn't really take his proposal seriously because by then I had even more reason to be very distrustful of men, even the seemingly kind and generous ones. I had been out in the world long enough to know how badly many of them treated their wives and girlfriends, the deceits they practised and the things they got up to when the opportunity arose. By then I was having a good time playing the field and certainly didn't want to pin all my hopes on one man. It was my view at that stage that a woman shouldn't pin her hopes on anyone but herself.

Joseph was a very good friend indeed, supporting me a great deal, and a man with whom I enjoyed spending time. I was very open with him about my life and he encouraged me to be there for Noel and to be kind to him. He showed no jealousy, which I thought demonstrated what a secure man he was and he thought that it was wonderful the way that I stayed by Noel. However, I knew better than to tell Noel about Joseph since Noel was beginning to show signs of possessiveness and jealousy which made me uneasy and unwilling to be as open with him about my life and my feelings as I could be with Joseph.

When I sold my studio flat in St John's Wood and persuaded Noel to top up this figure with enough money to buy the apartment in Alder Lodge, I used some of the money to buy a beautiful Jaguar XJS. It was a stunningly attractive car with fine lines and very easy on the eye. It was also a marque that I had fallen in love with when I had first seen it advertised. Although I had passed my driving test, I didn't actually drive and have only done so on one or two occasions in the past twenty years. I derive no pleasure from being behind the wheel but I thought that the car would be a lovely thing to own. The joy of owning beautiful and precious objects, be they cars, apartments, jewellery, clothes or anything else I find attractive is usually enough to satisfy me. I grew to like being surrounded by stylish and glamorous items, as they appealed to my sense of the aesthetic, and I liked the idea of keeping the Jaguar down in the garage so that men like Noel or Joseph could take me out in it when I wanted. Apart from not enjoying driving, I knew that I had a tendency to drive much too fast and, because of my social life, if I did choose to drive I was bound to have had too much champagne to be safe behind the wheel.

At this stage, between 1978 and 1980, I was still trying to maintain a relationship with my mother even though we weren't living together any longer. Joseph invited her and Paul, who was by now living with her, to dinner at the Grosvenor House one evening, saying that he wanted to meet someone who was such an important figure in my life. My mother and Paul behaved appallingly and when I was away from the table, Paul, having no shame at all, asked Joseph for money. It was not until a few days later that Joseph told me about the incident and I was absolutely mortified. He also told me that never before had he witnessed such jealousy from a mother towards a daughter.

'Your mother hates you,' he told me, 'I can sense it.'

When I told my mother that I knew of the request for money, she said that it had been all Paul's doing. 'You know how he drinks,' she said.

'Don't you dare ever do that again,' I said. 'It is embarrassing and cheap. Poverty is excusable, but lack of dignity is not.'

Even by my early twenties, I had gained a certain amount of experience in the arts of seduction but I was to learn a great deal more over the next twelve years or so and later became known as some sort of authority on the subject. One of the most exciting moments in the life of any woman is the first date. This is the time when being feminine, coquettish and adventurous comes into its own. It should be borne in mind that your date still does not know for certain why you accepted his invitation in the first place. He knows why he asked you, but he doesn't know for certain why you agreed, and this gives you the advantage.

When invited out to dine, I have always tried to find out in advance where I was going to be taken and when possible I would telephone the restaurant in order to ask them their dress code. It is very important that a woman be dressed appropriately for the occasion.

Once you have chosen that special little dress, have a last, admiring look in the mirror, and make any last-minute adjustments. These could be a ladder in your stockings, or hairs or powder that may have fallen on to your dress – always use a sticky roller to remove these. Put a little talcum powder in those essential stilettos. It is wonderfully absorbent, protects the shoes and allows confident foot games under the table. Make sure that your shoes are the last items you put on before leaving home and the last things you take off later.

One of the first rules, at any time, is not to keep your date waiting. You don't need to play childish games, delaying your appearance so as to heighten his anticipation. Behave from the outset as a lady. This is the manner in which you are used to being treated. If by any chance he is delayed, wait twenty-five minutes unless he has telephoned with an explanation. Conversely, if you find you are running late, telephone if possible. It is preferable to be met at home but it is also important to be considerate and flexible. Offer to meet him at a place of mutual convenience as you might be very far apart, in which case he should send a car to meet you.

Always give yourself a few minutes longer than are necessary to get ready and use them to check the final details. Always appear relaxed, as if you had spent the entire day preparing for the evening, even if you had to rush like mad. A man likes to feel that a woman has made a special effort for him.

On every occasion I have been taken out, regardless of the time of day, I have always sent a thank-you note. I might include some rose petals, but an exceptional occasion might arise, and in those circumstances I feel that something a little more special is appropriate. I normally settle for an orchid with a little note conveying my special message.

When a man and a woman are attracted to each other there is a fascinating dilemma: when to go to bed. Don't stifle spontaneity, but there is nothing more beautiful than the expression of love when two people have taken the trouble to get to know each other. When the fears and insecurities have been laid to rest and you feel entirely comfortable and relaxed together it will feel right. You are under no obligation to sleep with a man, no matter how giving he may have been. The waiting can enhance anticipation. The most passionate love affairs are those that remain unconsummated.

The act of lovemaking should be as exciting as a woman's personality. It should be adventurous, innovative and always pleasurable. It is one of the most intimate forms of self-expression and says everything about you. However, seduction is the first step. This you have already done by looking beautiful and suggestible. If he happens to be driving you home, insist on sitting in the back of his car and, using the type of vocabulary which he didn't even think you knew, excite him with your words and suggest what you might like him to do to you were he lucky enough to be in the back. Take him on a journey of sensuality, and bear in mind that the inadvertent sight of a little stocking-top is guaranteed to capture his attention as stockings indicate not only latent femininity and elegance but also a sense of sexual awareness.

Different locations are always exciting, so never be predictable. For a change of scenery, book into a luxurious hotel for that special occasion. To the surprise of the chambermaid I once took my own silk sheets to a hotel and insisted they be put on the bed before the arrival of my companion. After leaving the hotel I made a gift of the sheets to him as a very special birthday present for his *pied-à-terre*. But of course this can be limited to just the pillowcase.

It is also worthwhile considering an aeroplane, train or yacht. A woman should never feel limited by the more traditional locations for lovemaking, such as the bedroom. Or you could always try the boardroom or his office desk. Turn up unexpectedly with a bottle of chilled champagne and a wicked look. Buy a coffee-table book of the photographs of Helmut Newton or Bob Carlos Clarke and explore your fantasies together.

No woman can ever be beautiful unless a man makes her feel that way. You have to appeal to his taste and I always find it necessary to find out about his likes and dislikes. This extends over a wide range – from colours and scents to food and music. It is always exciting to a man to know that a woman has taken his preferences into consideration. This is seduction converted into an art form. The ultimate result of a successful seduction is not necessarily sexual. It is a question of winning over the man and appealing to all of his senses, for in the end this can form the basis for an exciting and beautiful relationship.

Part of the ability to win over a man's heart is to make him feel that he is the centre of your universe and the only one for you. One of the ways to do this is to listen attentively, gazing into his eyes and listening to his every word. Make him feel important by constantly asking for his views and opinions, be it on wines, food or anything that is of interest to him or is part of his work. I have found that most men are a little like peacocks: they like to shine and show off. Give him every chance, at least for the time being. Be patient, for your chance to take over will come later. For me one of the greatest pleasures, not to mention source of enlightenment, has been to spend time with men of intellect, influence and success. They are the greatest source of knowledge for the kind of woman who wishes to achieve something in her life. Over the years I got to learn not only about business but more importantly how it should be conducted. No woman can ever be successful or derive sustenance from a relationship unless she has the intelligence to make the most of every opportunity to learn. An intelligent woman has a magnetic attraction which is rarely to be found in someone who can only boast good looks. The combination of the two is quite devastating.

As far as your bedroom is concerned, every foray into your inner sanctum should be special and never routine. Creating the right atmosphere is essential. Candles, music and the scent of the room together set the right mood for the pleasures which are to follow. I used sometimes to like to place a single rose on my companion's pillow. The quality of the bed linen is very important. I prefer pure linen from Italy – Frette in Bond Street have the best – as it is finer than Irish linen or pure cotton. I sometimes use silk satin, also from Frette, but have always tried to avoid synthetic fibres. Talcum powder sprinkled on the sheets gives a wonderful softness to the skin and will remind you both of your childhood. There is something very special about the scent of Johnson's Baby Powder even though it is not officially recognized as an aphrodisiac.

On a hot night I would scatter frozen rose petals on the sheets, as the pleasure of lying on them is exquisite. Iced cologne on your back is also wonderfully refreshing. A way to initiate the sensual pleasures is to be relaxed. A gentle massage, starting with the feet and working your way up, caressing every part of the body and using light strokes at the top of the neck, is a good point from which to begin. You should be able to tell whether or not you are on the right track from his response. He will be thrilled if you initiate, so be bold, use your imagination and remember that lovemaking is the ultimate form of self-expression. You must always let him know what gives you pleasure. The act of asking is, in itself, very provocative. As the relationship progresses and you discover each other's needs you must explore your fantasies together.

All this knowledge was acquired over a long period of time and before

I arrived at the point where I could enjoy the fruits of my labour I had to work very hard. Noel and Joseph were both extremely generous to me and I returned their kindness by being an intelligent, stimulating and worthwhile companion over many years. However, soon after leaving Halcrow's I was determined to continue with my quest for success and I needed to think seriously about how to use my business experience to my best advantage. I still had the urge to work, because I wanted to make enough money to be completely independent of everyone. Noel was kindly paying my bills while I continued my studies and although I was now in a position to walk with great confidence into any shop, hotel or restaurant I chose, I still had a long way to go. My ideas on exactly what I was going to do were still rather nebulous at this stage. I thought that I might ultimately set myself up in public relations in some way, using my expanding circle of professional contacts, including the partners and prominent international clients of Halcrow's, as my client base. I had no intention of going into business blindly and with the financial help of men like Noel and Joseph; I didn't have to work until I was ready. After some thought I chose to attend St Godrick's College in Hampstead, where, after studying everything from management techniques to secretarial skills, I gained a degree in business administration. I also made a point of attending lectures and seminars at the Institute of Directors in Pall Mall. During this time I enjoyed a wonderful lifestyle and established a small group of close and trusted friends.

It is true to say that I had money, and access to more, but I was determined not to grab at it and then secretly hoard it away in a bank. I was going to use it to invest in myself and my future. I continued to see myself as a one-woman business and was still determined to make the most of all my assets. With Joseph and Noel continuing to be generous, it was my intention that with my knowledge of the business work and my well-placed contacts, I ought to start thinking seriously about how to make use of all of these. I concluded that I should combine them in such a way as to ensure that I could continue to live in an unapologetically luxurious style without necessarily having to rely on the kindness of my chosen consorts. It was my full intention to become the new Renaissance woman I had always set out to be, and now, with everything in place, I was going to do just that.

One evening over dinner, after taking me to see *Evita*, Andrew Lloyd Webber's musical based on the life of Eva Perón, Noel told me, 'You know, Bienvenida, you are a lot like her.' I still don't know if he meant it as a compliment or a subtle piece of criticism, but I was flattered that he should compare me to a woman of that ilk. He was still with his wife although he had intimated to me that it was his intention to divorce her and marry me. This, of course, was the last thing I wanted, and it never transpired. The problem with living so close to Noel was that he soon realized how playful I was and that I was seeing other men. In fact he became very childish about it and one day even sent me back all the gifts I had given him. He refused to speak to me for a while, but he loved me too much for his silence to last and as he wanted to continue to see me he was obliged to adapt to the new *status quo*. He had realized that I had no intention of changing my lifestyle just to please him, and his jealousy and possessiveness soon passed.

5

Application

I have always considered clothes to be one of the most important parts of a successful woman's armoury. Even as a child I was fascinated by the shops, magazines and films in which I saw an entire array of women's clothes which, although not of the quality which I was later to acquire, were certainly an improvement on the drab, colourless dresses and skirts worn by the majority of women in my neighbourhood.

As a child I was always well turned out and presentable, but my wardrobe was limited and I remember gazing with ill-concealed awe at my mother's clothes as she packed and unpacked her neat and tidy suitcases on her visits to Spain.

As a young girl I was never the 'jeans and T-shirt' type – I thought they looked scruffy – and as I had fine features and beautiful hair I didn't see any reason to hide myself among crowds of people all wearing the same instantly forgettable clothes. As soon as I had access to money I was able to start buying designer names. I was influenced by Italian, French and American fashion magazines and I knew the names, styles and cuts of all the top couturiers but more through appreciation of their creations than an urge to own them. I have always been fond of the work of classic designers such as Chanel, Balenciaga and Vionnet, but when I arrived in London I was still a few years away from being able to indulge my passion for these lofty and seemingly unattainable names. Instead I relied on my ability as a seamstress to alter and adapt clothes, bought with money that I had saved, from boutiques in Oxford Street and from Marks & Spencer. In this regard I had a good deal of flair and imagination and was able, with the right accessories, to turn them into something special, developing my own distinctive style as I went along. With the advent of financial backing and therefore the ability to go abroad and wear what I wanted rather than what I could afford, I spread my wings further than the sartorial limitations of London and sought clothes in New York, Paris, Milan and elsewhere.

Through travel, my taste in clothes developed, and because I found the fashions of London too trendy, fleeting and shapeless, I sought more elegant and classic lines in the great fashion houses of which I had seen pictures in my youth. I wanted elegance, style, imagination and, most importantly, femininity from the clothes I wore, and in London I was able to find many lovely items in the Bond Street shops Régine and Crocodile.

Perfume and beauty treatments were also very important to me and I always made sure that my bathroom and dressing-room were well stocked with a wide selection of delicately scented soaps and perfumes and that all my drawers had their own scent bags to keep the clothes smelling fresh. I particularly liked Calèche, a classic perfume by Hermès, because when I was a young girl my mother used to bring me samples of it on her visits to Valencia. In that respect, as well as clothes, she had very good taste and I can only imagine that she was open-minded enough to have been influenced by the ladies for whom she worked.

Looking back on it now, it all sounds rather easy, as if all I had to do was to smile sweetly at a few rich men and be showered with fabulous gifts. In reality it was not like that at all. To be a good companion and friend to an older man is not always fun. There were, of course, the compensations of enjoying a glamorous lifestyle, but I had, in return, to work very hard to make sure they were happy. There are times when an age gap of twenty or thirty years can seem more than the generation it actually is and in terms of taste, preferences, attitudes and values the disparity can be enormous. Noel, for example, had different tastes from me in most things and a lifetime of experiences which I was totally unable to appreciate. Not because I wasn't interested but because it all seemed so terribly alien to me. He would often talk at length about the war, a subject that can become rather depressing for a young girl. But, however bored I was, I would always remain kind and patient because it was my perception that this was my side of an unspoken arrangement at which we had arrived.

Occasionally it can be hard to deal with people who have become set in their ways and are permanently used to getting exactly what they want. I don't want to imply that their opinions and attitudes are in any way wrong but the older people become, the less flexible seem to be their views and vision. To build a successful relationship with a powerful older man, a woman has to seem to dedicate herself to him completely when she is in his company. I remember, when I went to see *Evita* with Noel, I developed the most excruciating stomach cramps. However, knowing how much he had been looking forward to the show, I kept very quiet and managed to ignore the pain so as not to ruin his evening.

Men are often as difficult and as petulant as children, and they have to be indulged and spoiled much of the time if they are not to become cantankerous. Just like children, their characters vary enormously: some can be charming and warm despite their faults, while others become ruthless, pompous and overbearing yet fascinating nonetheless. Any woman, young or old, wanting to befriend such a man has to put up with every mood, whim and caprice, learning as much as she can about the subjects and issues which interest that individual, be it engineering, politics, art, music or high finance, and then allowing him to indulge himself in being as boring as he likes when he has had too much to drink or merely get carried away on a wave of his own conceit and memories. There are many times when you have to just let him talk, allowing him to share his thoughts and feelings without arguing, criticizing or judging him as might someone of his own generation. That is the role of a friend and true companion.

Busy men also become tired of always eating in restaurants and so I ensured that in my capacity as a companion, and also as a seduction technique, I extended my abilities to the dining-room, learning to cook and create meals that fulfilled a man's wildest and most extravagant fantasies when I entertained at home.

I was obliged to teach myself everything, since the sort of food I had eaten as a child would hardly be likely to captivate and intrigue the kind of men I now wanted to spoil. The most important thing is that everything should go smoothly and without any apparent effort, so I have always avoided potential complications, preferring simplicity, and served the highest-quality ingredients with perfect presentation. I always have chilled champagne ready when a guest arrives, although I must say, as a genuine lover of the grape in its effervescent form, that this is just as much for me, on a day-to-day basis, as for anyone else. The crystal glasses are always chilled, too, for maximum impact and effect: this adds a certain delicacy to the experience, exciting the fingertips and tantalizing the lips even before the champagne itself has touched them. I make a point of never keeping my guests waiting while I cook or prepare food as everything is carefully made ready in advance. I certainly wouldn't want them to see me flustered and working away in the kitchen, opening and shutting the oven with an apron over my dress and carrying with me the smells that should be reserved for the kitchen itself.

I am always flamboyant in the way I present the food as I feel that a meal should not be simply an Epicurean pleasure but a visual one as well. Now that I have a husband who is an excellent cook I tend to spend less and less time in the kitchen, which has become his exclusive domain. In the past, however, I learnt how to prepare and present most straightfoward dishes as well as a few complicated ones. Needless to say, there have been numerous occasions when a lunch or dinner I was hosting and/or preparing was for close friends and very informal and relaxed. At such times I was quite capable of producing less elaborate meals but for my dinner parties and intimate, romantic and more seductive evenings with a distinct intention in mind, I truly pulled out all the stops.

The finest caviar in the world is Iranian Gold, closely followed by Beluga, either of which I used to buy at the Caviar House in Geneva. Of course, the preparing of this delicacy is minimal but the presentation is paramount. I would always serve it in a beautiful Lalique crystal bowl and instead of putting it on ice I would use dry ice, adding water just before serving, so that the dark and luscious little eggs would be swathed in bewitching clouds of smoke as they came to the candle-lit table, which itself was decorated with the giant, exuberant white Casablanca lilies I love so much. I then might serve smoked salmon, very thinly cut, sprinkled with chopped dill and accompanied with half lemons wrapped in black tulle with a gold bow so that when they are squeezed the pips don't jump into the food; this arrangement I affectionately refer to as 'nappies'. Instead of caviar, I might serve game consommé with lightly poached quails' eggs, or with gold leaf floating on the surface to create a mood of decadent luxury. Sometimes I would bake sea bass and bring it to the table with dried herbs such as rosemary, which I would burn in front of my guest to create an exquisite aroma. In other occasions I might fill half a melon with cranberries steeped in liqueur and then wrap the whole thing in cellophane tied with bows of gold wire, rather like expensive chocolates. I love asparagus *al dente*, bound together with straw bows as a bed for quails' eggs ... The list of delicacies which the world has to offer is endless, and fine foods need not be swamped in complicated and intricate sauces which only succeed in overpowering their delicate taste and leave a dish *trop cuisiné*.

I believe that everything in life, down to the most mundane details, should be done in a beautiful and dramatic way, if it is at all possible, with consummate thought and effort put into both preparation and presentation. Men don't fall in love with a woman just because of the way she looks and dresses and if they do it is a very shallow, short-lived and usually insincere reaction. They also are enamoured by the way she behaves and the environment she creates around them. I knew for a fact that whenever I invited a man to dinner he would always feel a strong desire to return since no one else would be able to give him such a perfect experience.

I still keep a file of recipes to which I add whenever I come across one I like in a magazine, as I always used to, even though my husband now takes care of virtually all the cooking. I have always watched carefully how food was prepared and presented in the best hotels and restaurants in the world. When I was staying in a private house or on a yacht where there was a chef in residence, I would make a point of spending time in the kitchen, hunting out new ideas, asking questions and discussing recipes. Food, like music and art, all of which I enjoy for their sensual dividends, should be considered on equal terms with any of the delights for the other four senses.

A final suggestion: I have always kept a carefully annotated file in which I write the likes and dislikes of my guests – their interests, hobbies, family details and even their pet's name as well as a few more intimate and interesting details – and whenever I gave a reception or dinner I could refer to this *aide-mémoire*.

It might be assumed, now that I had gained my independence from my mother, that I would be rid of all her unpleasantness, but this was not the case. The desire for approval from one's parents is incredibly strong, no matter how great the indifference a good many people try to display. Indeed I still felt some pangs of guilt that perhaps in some small way I had been responsible for our inability to coexist in an atmosphere of harmony. Thus I maintained our relationship and, having moved to Alder Lodge in Fulham, I invited her to the flat in an effort to patch things up. At that time she was working at the Charing Cross Hospital. I was not trying to impress her with my home or possessions; rather I had a sincere wish to work out our problems. 'You don't have to work any more,' I told her proudly. 'I would be very happy to look after you.'

'Well,' she said, 'I would be very happy to give up work as long as you are sure you can take care of me and my welfare.'

'Of course I will look after you,' I repeated, without quite realizing exactly what she meant. She went on to explain that she would want me to compensate her for her pension, the benefits of her insurance policies and everything else that she would be giving up if she were to leave her job. I agreed to her demands but it seemed that nothing I ever gave her was enough and she always ended up complaining. I would take her shopping with me, buying her jewellery and even a fur coat, but she was constantly accusing me behind her back of being mean. On one occasion when I had my wisdom teeth removed, I asked her to be with me in case I felt dizzy after the injections and needed help. I asked her to bring me some Cox's apples, which, though probably inappropriate at the time, I loved to eat. She brought the apples but, even though they cost only a few pence in those days, asked me to pay for them, giving the impression that I might be trying to take advantage of her in some way.

'But I'm your daughter,' I said, aghast. 'I've had an unpleasant operation and you're going to make me pay for a few apples?'

'You have the money and I don't!' she snapped.

Years later I learnt that over the years she had, in fact, accumulated quite a little fortune.

However carefully we prepare our plans and strategies it is often pure luck that creates the biggest chances in our lives, but luck can be capitalized upon only by those who make sure they are in the right place at the right time. In 1977 I was very close to Noel and he was providing most of the support I needed to press ahead with my various courses and get on with developing myself as a person. But I was not content with simply being a kept woman and this was certainly not the be-all and end-all of my ambitions. I was not independent and my plans to become so not yet under way. I needed to meet more powerful and affluent people and then make use of them so that I could move even further forward and create an ever-bigger network of contacts. As far as I was concerned, the ball had rolled a little bit then stopped, and I wanted to get it rolling again.

If I'd been obliged to continue working full-time I would not have been able to take as many courses in different subjects or to meet as many people socially. The majority of people in the world of commerce never achieve as much as they might because at the end of the working day they have neither the energy nor the inclination to develop other areas of expertise in order to progress both socially and professionally.

Noel had freed me from those shackles and had been happy for me to leave Halcrow's and be more available to him. I was awaiting my opportunity to work in some sort of consultancy capacity for him and preparing myself for the role. As far as I was concerned, the company had merely been the first rung on the ladder to realizing my ambitions. When Noel told me that he had a business meeting in Morocco I thought that I should go along, although not in any official capacity. I had not travelled much at that stage and it sounded like an interesting opportunity to start exploring the world. Noel's meeting was in Rabat, where he would be staying with his secretary and other people from Halcrow's. It would not have been appropriate for me to be with him officially, or to stay in the same hotel, as I was no longer with the company. So I invited Maria, a Portuguese friend in her early thirties, whom I had met in London, to come with me as a sort of chaperone-cum-companion to the tiny resort of Mohammedia, on the coast between Casablanca and Rabat. I very much liked the feeling of being able to invite someone and pay for them as my guest.

As well as being a resort town, Mohammedia is also a centre for oil refineries. The Moroccan Airlines office recommended the Mohammedia Hotel as the best five-star hotel in the area, so I booked a suite of rooms overlooking the swimming-pool, with the glittering Mediterranean just beyond. It was all very beautiful and exciting. I was twenty and this was the first time I had been away from London as a free and semi-independent woman. I felt that I had already achieved a certain amount in just a few years and I was ambitious to achieve a great deal more. Now I was in a strong position to start building a career.

The airline had advised me well and the hotel boasted a fine guest list full of interesting and well-connected people. There were two dangerous-seeming brothers from Lebanon to whom Maria and I talked a good deal, and a charming, elegant and dignified young man who was the Emir of Mauritania and always had his head buried in a book whenever we saw him wandering around the hotel. I was learning a tremendous amount from this variety of men and beginning to be able to distinguish the honourable ones from those that seemed to bluff their way through life. So many men, I was discovering, are full of boasts and promises when they are talking to women, eager to impress with their big talk of how successful they are or soon will be, how huge deals are just over the horizon and what close friends they are with other rich, powerful or famous people. Sometimes it is as if they actually believe what they are saying themselves and many of them are very convincing and highly persuasive. No doubt this is how they manage to survive, bluffing their way through the years in the hope that one day they will strike lucky. But most of them never amount to anything, because when the luck does come their way they don't know how to either recognize or capitalize on it. The difficulty for young and naïve women is knowing which men are genuine and which are not. At that stage I had little to lose apart from time wasted listening to them, because it would have taken a great deal more to influence me than a few words spoken over a drink or two.

Maria and I were in the bar of the hotel before lunch one day when a great opportunity presented itself. We were both elegantly dressed and quite the centre of attention. A distinguished-looking Middle Eastern gentleman in his late thirties, wearing a black business suit and tie, came over to talk to us. He spoke in French, introducing himself as Mohammed. Maria, whose French was a great deal less rusty than mine, did most of the talking, all of which I was able to follow.

'Are you staying in the hotel?' we asked, making polite conversation.

'No,' he answered, 'I am here on business, visiting one of the oil refineries. I just wanted to have a drink so I came to the hotel.'

We went on to explain that we were on holiday but that I was also there because of my employer, who was the senior partner in a UK engineering consultancy called Sir William Halcrow & Partners.

'Oh yes,' he nodded, 'I have heard of them. I work with the Moroccan Ministry of Oil and the Minister of Energy and Mines, Moussa Saadi, is a close friend of mine. We are considering building underwater pipelines from Gibraltar and southern Spain to Morocco. Perhaps there is something here that we could discuss. Will you join me for lunch?'

He took us both for lunch in the hotel restaurant and during the meal he invited us to a party at the Minister's summer-house in Rabat that evening.

'There will be many important people at the party,' he said, 'and I could introduce you to the Minister.'

We were delighted to accept. 'We will order a taxi to take us over,' I said. 'That will be all right, won't it?'

'I wouldn't use one of the local taxis to go out across the desert,' Mohammed warned, 'in case it breaks down. There is a great danger for young Western women from kidnappers and bandits. You would be better off hiring a private car with a driver. You will be much safer and much more comfortable.' So that afternoon I ordered a Mercedes and driver to pick us up from the hotel. I was grateful to Mohammed for his advice and felt much relieved at the thought of arriving at the party in comfort and style.

The sun was just setting over the sand dunes as we sped through the dramatic, desolate landscape in the dark-blue, air-conditioned car. It was like being lifted out of the ordinary world and being placed in a cocoon of calm, comfort and security, a cool bubble humming through the heat, dust and potholes of real life. We drove for nearly an hour and a half. I was wearing a Moroccan kaftan which I had bought in Casablanca. Black with specks of gold, it looked very dramatic with my blonde hair, and I thought that it would be courteous to wear a long dress like that. I didn't want to be trendy – I wanted to be timelessly elegant. We were elated and curious about the party and intrigued by the mystery of that beautiful country.

The house in Rabat was a white-walled palace, sitting amid gardens, fountains and ponds, a fragrant oasis from the urban bustle outside. We drew up between the rows of limousines and I was very relieved not to be getting out of some battered old taxi and haggling with a scruffy driver, as the other guests drifted past calm and immaculate. There was an intoxicating scent in the air as the jasmine flowers woke up for the night. We climbed the steps, passed through the columns of the arched entrance, past the liveried doorman, to be greeted by smiling servants in kaftans and curly-toed slippers who offered us glasses of sweet mint tea from trays. It was like entering a completely different world, where every wall and inch of floor was covered in the most beautiful and intricate mosaics. The evening was very cool and I fancied I could hear the sound of running water from the central fountain even though there was a band playing and a gentle buzz of animated conversation. Silk cushions were laid out on which some guests sat, while others were moving around talking and laughing with one another. Tables bore exquisite and delicate food and fruit, and people were helping themselves or being assisted by the servants.

Mohammed saw us arrive and strode across the room to greet us, looking very elegant in a white kaftan with wide sleeves. We were beautifully treated, and people felt comfortable enough to come up and talk to us with no need for introductions. I have always been puzzled in England that people who go to social gatherings often seem frightened and timid, lacking the confidence to strike up a conversation with others. I do not understand why they go to parties if they feel that insecure; it must be such agony for them to have to force themselves to mix. It's not the same in other countries. I have always felt very comfortable with Arabs and people from the Middle East, probably because of my Spanish heritage. We have, after all, been historically linked with them for more than six hundred years. They are gracious and elegant people who know how to live well.

Mohammed told us that his friend and our host for the evening, the Minister of Energy and Mines, was eager to meet us. 'I have told him all about you,' he confessed with a twinkle, as he took us over and introduced us. Moussa Saadi was a tall, distinguished man in his late forties. He had piercing eyes and a grey beard and was dressed in a Western suit as if he had come straight from a business meeting. We talked for a while and drank champagne. I told him about my connection with Halcrow's and that Noel was in Rabat.

'I would be very interested in meeting Mr Cochrane while he is out here,' he said. 'Would you like to bring him to lunch with me?'

This was exactly the sort of work I wanted to do for Noel, meeting people and introducing them to him. I felt wonderful to know that I could actually provide a contact which would be useful to both the Minister and Noel. It seemed so obvious and easy – just a question of being in the right place at the right time and having the ability to impress people with my understanding of the matters at hand. The rest of the evening was perfect, but Maria and I ended up staying, just the two of us, in a suite at the Rabat Hilton as the guests of the Minister, rather than returning to Mohammedia that night, as it was very late by the time the party finally wound down. As I went to bed I felt almost light-headed with pleasure and not at all tired. I was determined to contact Noel at the first possible moment and ask him if he would like me to go ahead with arranging the meeting.

Noel was just as interested in the idea of meeting the Minister as I had anticipated. Even if this particular deal came to nothing they would still be able to forge a connection which could be built upon at a later date. I glowed with pride when he told me how enterprising I was to have been able to bring about such an introduction. More than anything I wanted him to appreciate that I was intelligent and able to work at the same level as him. I could tell he was impressed with me and that was a very good feeling. I arranged for us all to meet for lunch in Casablanca, where the Minister's office was. Mohammed recommended a restaurant where we all sat on low benches in the traditional style. I kept very quiet and wore a kaftan again, out of respect for my host. I was listening and watching everything around me, studying their behaviour so that I could learn for any future such occasions. I needed to be able to adapt to any situation, no matter what the cultural setting, that called for an understanding of etiquette.

As I listened to them talk and thought about the way they did business I began to see how I was going to build my business career. I realized that the way these people became rich and successful was by working as middlemen in huge international deals. If someone needed a motorway or a container port built, a new airport designed or a hospital planned, a new source of oil or equipment for an invading army, then millions of pounds would be changing hands. Anyone who became part of the process, taking even a small percentage along the way, was likely to become rich as a result. No matter what these people might call themselves, be it agents, representatives, consultants, public-relations experts or liaison officers, their skills lay in introducing two parties who could do business together and then taking a fee or a percentage from either or both. Anyone who can provide the first link in the chain, the first introduction and recommendation, is worth an enormous amount of money to those companies – indeed a sum completely out of proportion to the actual degree of time spent and effort involved in making the contact. It might take only a few minutes for the middlemen to plan out what to do and a few days to arrange the necessary meeting, but the outcome might well result in the redirecting of millions of pounds to a chosen contractor or supplier and the payment of a few hundred thousand pounds, to a middleman for setting the ball rolling.

It was a realization towards which I had been working for some time, but now the whole picture was crystal-clear to me. The skill of the middlemen, I now understood, lay in being there to smooth the way for the big banks, investors and companies selling services like construction and engineering or products like oil and machinery. I was learning that there was a market in bringing people together for business purposes and I thought I could exploit it. Hadn't I done just that for Noel and the Minister? Why should I not be able to do it again and again, for any number of people? I decided that the way forward was to continue getting to know influential people so that when opportunities arose to make introductions, I would be in a position to benefit. It was all going to be a question of personal relationships and I knew that this was something at which I could become very, very good.

After my visit to Morocco I became increasingly aware of the different possibilities offered by the people I met and clearer about what I was looking for in relationships. I was constantly on the lookout for people who might benefit from my presence and influence and always happy to accept invitations to any gatherings that might be conducive to my business needs.

I was soon to meet a man called Michael, a contact of Noel's, and a wealthy Saudi Arabian called Ahmed. Michael, an Englishman, was the manager of Ahmed's petrochemical company in the Middle East. The party at which we met was very elegant, with all sorts of people coming and going throughout the evening, all of them potential contacts with whom I ought to mingle and get to know.

A few weeks after the party I received a call from Michael. 'Ahmed was very taken by you,' he explained after the usual exchange of politeness, 'and asked me to ring you to ask if you would consider doing us a favour.'

'What sort of favour?' I asked with growing curiosity.

'We would like you to take a sample of glass-reinforced plastic to Bahrain because we are thinking of testing it for a piping project in Saudi Arabia.' I knew from working at Halcrow's that this material had been used for the first time successfully in the dome of the airport in Sharja which the company had built for the government of the United Arab Emirates. The material was particularly suitable for the Middle East because it could expand and contract without cracking as a result of the fluctuations that normally accompanied the extreme changes in temperature which occur in the desert. It was a very innovative product. 'We realize,' Michael continued, 'that it would be difficult or a single woman to go to Saudi alone and we suggest that we meet you in Bahrain.'

'I would be delighted to do this for you,' I said, thinking that it would be an interesting adventure and challenge as well as an opportunity to increase the number of my contacts. I was also well aware of what Michael had meant when he'd said that Ahmed had been very taken with me. I knew that the state of Bahrain was altogether a more tolerant and westernized place than Saudi and that I could expect to be shown great hospitality. The islands had been the first of the Gulf States to find oil in 1932 and had therefore had plenty of time to acclimatize to their wealth. Bahrain was well known for its generous welfare system, as well as for new industries like oil refining and ship repairing. It was also a banking, communications and tax-free entry port for the entire region – just the sort of place where middlemen congregated to do their deals.

'Good,' said Michael, sounding genuinely pleased. 'We have arranged your ticket and if you go to the Bahraini Embassy in London we will sponsor you for your visa.'

Noel, to whom I had relayed the plan, was very proud of me and liked the idea that I was doing something with my life at a commercial level, but I was aware that he was becoming rather jealous and possessive of me and at an emotional level wanted to keep me entirely to himself. While I was very fond of him and grateful for all the opportunities with which he had presented me, I did not intend to devote my whole life to him. Apart from anything else, he still had a wife and family and was therefore in no position to demand fidelity from me. Therefore I did not believe I should feel guilty about keeping secrets from him, either now or at any time in the future, especially if I could spare him any hurt by withholding information. We were both free people, capable of leading our own lives.

I took a taxi to the embassy, just off Gloucester Road, with my first-class ticket and the name of my sponsors, but the official at the desk shook his head and told me that I didn't have the right paperwork. Being smartly and expensively dressed, I was clearly making an impression on the staff, who could see that they were not dealing with the usual type of business traveller. Because of the importance of my sponsor, the matter was brought to the attention of the Ambassador and before I knew it I had been summoned to his office on the first floor. As I was shown in he rose from his desk. Ali Al Mahroos was a short man, about forty or perhaps a bit older, and a little chubby, but very smart and dignified. There seemed to be an immediate chemistry between us and after we had been talking for only a few minutes it was as if we had known each other for years. He offered me coffee and as we chatted he invited me for a drink that evening, an invitation which I was happy to accept.

'I'm going to have dinner with a very dear friend of mine this evening, Ahmed Kano,' he told me. 'I would very much like to take you with me if you are available.'

I didn't realize it then, but Kano was one of the richest men in the Middle East, coming from an old trading family of Jewish origin which had established itself so deeply in Bahrain that it was almost like a royal family. In London he lived in an enormous house in Farm Street, Mayfair, and it was there that the Ambassador and I arrived that evening in the Ambassador's official car. The house was furnished with the finest antiques, paintings and *objets d'art*, including a big, discreetly lit Rubens in the drawing-room, and elaborate flower arrangements everywhere. It was a beautiful and extremely tasteful house and I couldn't help but be impressed. In the dining-room there was a beautiful marble table, reflected a hundred times in the mirrors which covered the ceiling. Servants brought caviar and smoked salmon to us, and Kano, the Ambassador and I talked. Kano was a slim, short man of about sixty, balding but very elegant and dignified.

After a couple of hours, despite the fact that the house had its own full-sized discotheque in the basement, Kano changed from the white robe he had been wearing into a suit and the three of us went around the corner to Annabel's in Berkeley Square for dinner. I had been there before and knew that it was the most fashionable nightclub in London. During the evening I became increasingly impressed by the quiet power and style of Kano. He was obviously a man of great quality and it made me feel good just to be with him as he had the dignity and elegant manners to be expected in a person of his background and calibre.

'Would you like to dance with me?' he asked after we had been there some time.

'Of course,' I replied, delighted that he had asked me, and once we were on the dance floor he asked me for my telephone number. I felt it would have been more appropriate if I had asked the Ambassador first before I gave it to him as it was he who had invited me in the first place, so I tried to stall. 'I can't really write it down here,' I said.

'Just tell it to me,' he smiled. 'I will remember it.'

The evening was wonderful and it ended after we left Annabel's, with the Ambassador taking me home with nothing further ado. But somehow

I felt sure that I would be seeing Kano again; I certainly hoped so.

A few days later the Bahraini Embassy rang to tell me that a visa would be waiting for me in Manama. I was aware that there was a risk attached to accepting this sort of assurance: there was always the possibility that I might arrive after a long flight only to find that no one knew anything about me and I would then be bundled unceremoniously on to the first flight out. But I decided to take a chance and flew out two days later, with the sample of reinforced plastic piping in my luggage. Ahmed and Michael were waiting for me at the airport and I was taken immediately to the Sheraton Hotel, where I learnt, not really to my surprise, that I was to be staying with Ahmed. They told me that I should order whatever I wanted from room service or eat in any of the restaurants and that the bill would be taken care of.

I stayed on the island for several days, spending my afternoons exploring the souks with a driver and in the evenings going out with Ahmed, Michael and a Moroccan girl. At that time Concorde had just started in commercial service and was flying only between Bahrain and London pending granting of permission for it to serve other destinations. The publicity surrounding these inaugural flights went a long way to raising Bahrain in the international consciousness and encouraging the international business community to visit the island. It was a shrewd public relations move. I had followed the progress of Concorde throughout its trials and loved the design of the sleek piece of modern technological and aerodynamic engineering. The idea of so much speed and elegance excited me. I talked about it to Ahmed and Michael and asked if I could go back to England on it. Ahmed smiled and nodded, apparently amused to be able to indulge my fantasy, and my ticket was changed accordingly. I was later to fly on Concorde on numerous other occasions and the experience was to become one of my truly great self-indulgent passions.

There were only twelve other passengers on that flight and I felt very privileged to think that I was flying at twice the speed of sound when I was still only twenty-one even though I had earned the right to do so. I had come a long way from my miserable childhood and that never-ending train journey over the mountains from Valencia to Gijón. In just one decade, and of my volition, I had jumped from the age of steam to that of super-sonic flight. My life was taking off with the same force as the great aeroplane in which I was so comfortably seated. I was learning how to use my femininity and intelligence to make men of stature fall for me, just as it had always been my intention. I liked the feeling of being valued for myself, and the approval I was being shown, and I intended to more than compensate for the lack of such approval in my early years. Despite the intimacy, there had been no emotional connection between me and Ahmed in Bahrain and I had looked upon the whole venture as no more than a challenging and interesting job. All I had really done was act as a courier. However, it was my first assignment and I had charged Michael for the time that I had spent carrying out that task and had been very well rewarded.

I returned to London and resumed my life as a social butterfly, always on the lookout for opportunities for useful contacts, keeping my ear to the ground and picking up snippets of information here and there, constantly searching out people for whom I felt I might be able to engineer deals.

I continued to educate myself and read avidly. Over time I was to learn of men that the very kindest and nicest ones were often not the most powerful, not the billionaires and the great leaders, who are too worried about themselves all the time, but the financially secure and successful senior executives, lawyers and doctors. The fact first crystallized in my mind when I was watching the 1958 film *Gigi*, when the young girl played by Leslie Caron is being taught how to be a courtesan by her aunt, played by Hermione Gingold, who has been the lover of many great men. The aunt is showing Gigi all the jewels she has collected over the years from the men she has known. Gigi picks up something very beautiful and asks if it was a present from a prince. The aunt answers something along the lines of: 'No, my dear, a prince doesn't feel that he has to give a woman anything because the fact that he is there at all he considers a gift.' A perceptive comment which was to help me focus on my ambitions and target with even greater deliberation the men that I deemed appropriate.

Although I am associated in the public mind with the older of my stream of companions, I have also enjoyed the company of men somewhat closer to my own age. But while there have been many admirers who were youthful and handsome to whom I may have been attracted, I resisted the temptation to develop relationships with any of them on the grounds that the rewards would not have outweighed the outlay of my time. Many women stay with handsome young men because they make them look good, but I wanted to satisfy other needs. I wanted to be with men who could appreciate a person of my calibre and look upon me as an investment. Young men don't have the time for any of that, as they are too busy building their own lives, and I knew that if I didn't make a life of my own, sooner or later I would end up a loser, clinging on desperately to some husband who didn't love me any more, just to maintain some financial stability. And I had no intention of ever letting that happen.

Shortly after I arrived back from Bahrain, Ali, the Bahraini Ambassador, phoned me and invited me out again. I was delighted to hear from him and in time we became very close as well as good friends. He was very kind and generous and in time introduced me to a number of very useful contacts. On our first date he arrived at my apartment with a beautiful silver ice bucket from Asprey and throughout our time together I made sure that he never let such generosity falter.

Within weeks of my becoming involved with Ali, British Airways telephoned me to say that a first-class ticket had been purchased for me to return to Bahrain.

'Purchased by whom?' I asked.

'We don't have a name,' the caller said. 'We just have a prepaid ticket for you.'

I was aware that Kano owned most of the travel agencies on the island and I suspected that the ticket might have been arranged by him. If so, it was a very exciting prospect, for I had thought about him a certain amount since meeting him that one night in Mayfair, and somehow felt that having coincidentally been to Bahrain and become familiar with it, I was destined to get to know him better. My visa was still valid, so I didn't have to go back to the embassy or mention the trip to Ali. I didn't think that it would be appropriate for him to know that a man to whom he had introduced me might now be courting me. There was also no reason to tell Noel about any of these developments unless I encountered situations where people were looking for a firm of consulting engineers, and anyway it was my personal life and I didn't feel that I needed to account to anyone for my movements.

As I had a young friend called Dawn who I knew was looking for an unattached man and who was fascinated by my way of life, I asked her if she would like to come with me to Bahrain as a travelling companion. This was a generous and extravagant gesture which I was to repeat many times over the years with a number of different girlfriends. When we arrived at the hotel I received a note from Kano confirming my suspicion that he was behind the trip and inviting me to a party at his home. Unfortunately the invitation didn't include Dawn and she became furiously jealous. Our relationship did not recover from that point on and I realized that I had made a serious mistake in inviting her. There is always the danger that if you carry other people along with you they will slow you down at the critical moment. And so I was very much afraid that Dawn's grumbling, her lack of opportunistic vision and intelligence would become detrimental to me and I was not going to miss out on this opportunity just because she didn't want to spend the evening alone.

Kano's house in Bahrain was palatial. It was partly Italianate in style, with Venetian chandeliers and paintings, very elegant and unusual in design and very different from the Farm Street house, with its heavy curtains and eighteenth-century gilt furniture. Here the clean, modern lines were much more to my taste than all the fussiness of the Mayfair mansion. As I walked into the party I was horrified to see Ali standing talking to a small group of men. It had not been my intention to hurt him and I became concerned about his feelings since he had always shown me such kindness and was obviously very fond of me. I didn't like the idea of hurting him and spoiling our friendship, or possibly damaging his relationship with his friend Kano. But to my utter relief, it became apparent that he'd known of my intended visit all along and even smiled as we met.

'I am so sorry,' I said, not knowing how to look at him. He was very understanding and forgiving and I came to realize that Middle Eastern etiquette demanded that he had to step down and give me up to the more powerful and older man however much this might hurt him. In return it would give him a lot of prestige in Kano's eyes to have made the gesture and would thus cement their friendship further. This was the last time I was to see Ali and I did miss his company when I returned to London. Once I realized that he was going to be gracious about my presence at the party, I started to circulate and discovered that there were other people there who were also influential figures in Bahrain, including the rulers of the country as well as bankers and businessmen. It was to prove a useful evening and instinctively I knew that once again luck had smiled on me and I was in the right place at the right time. Kano was very charming, the perfect host, and invited me to come back the next day on my own to visit another house which he owned on the island.

The following morning his limousine came to the hotel to pick me up and transport me to his house on the beach.

'You are making a fool of yourself,' sniffed Dawn as I prepared to go out. I didn't bother to reply, but just smiled as sweetly as I could. Although she was annoying me, I was beginning to feel a little sorry for her. However, I didn't want to be distracted by her and anyway she was to leave a few days later, whisked out of the country to the Far East by a man whom she was just about to meet. This was to the first of many disappointments with female travelling companions and friends, and I was never to see her again.

As I was driven through the gates of the house, the guards smiled and bowed their heads to the vehicle, making me feel very welcome if not highly important. The house was the most spectacular place, with acres of immaculate rose gardens reaching down to the private beach. Kano greeted me politely and warmly and immediately began showing me around the lawns, terraces and greenhouses, as proud of his possessions as if he had been a little boy showing me his toys. We sat taking aromatic tea as the gardeners and sprinklers worked quietly around us. The heat caused the flowers to add their own perfumes to the warm air as we sat deep in conversation, enjoying the fine sunshine.

'Would you like to see around my home?' Kano asked.

'I should be delighted to,' I replied.

Inside the house he showed me some of his treasures. In one cabinet he had a ship carved entirely out of rosewood and, because it had been worked from the heart of the tree, the scent was almost overwhelming as he opened the glass doors. There were flowers everywhere from the gardens in all the rooms, including the dining-room, where the table had been set for two with gold cutlery and the finest porcelain. Kano courteously placed me at the head of the table and sat down to my right. Servants kept bringing exquisite *hors'd-oeuvres*, followed by wonderful shellfish and cold Dom Pérignon and as we ate and drank he talked about his flowers, his home and his interests. He had a magnificent collection of Lalique glass which was to inspire me to form a collection of my own when I returned to England.

After lunch he took me upstairs to his bedroom. It was a lovely peach-coloured room, with the bed facing a window offering views over the balcony and across the blue ocean beyond. The bathroom was grey marble, with a Jacuzzi and a steam room. When I opened the wooden doors to the vanity unit I saw that he had a bottle of every perfume imaginable. Whatever scent a woman could want, he had in there. I was later to discover that he had the same range of scents in his bedroom at the house in Farm Street, behind a panelled wall. I was not remotely fazed that the perfume suggested that a large number of women had probably seen the same selection. Neither of us was pretending that the encounter was anything other than it was and we spent a pleasant enough afternoon. That evening, as I was about to be driven home, Kano gave me a beautiful bouquet of red and yellow roses from the garden.

Back in London after my trip, I reflected that it had been fruitful in two ways: as well as meeting Kano I had engineered some more useful introductions. Things were going to plan.

Kano rang me some time later and we resumed our affair. We met regularly from then on, although there were some gaps of two or three months between meetings because he was so busy travelling. Once, after he had enjoyed an intimate evening with me, I remember him saying, 'You have a unique ability, Bienvenida, to make a man feel like a man.' I thought that very flattering. When he was in London we used to go to Les Ambassadeurs together and to Annabel's, where I was by now regarded as a member. I always used to be given the best table, number ten, which was close to the dance floor but behind a glass partition and therefore quite intimate. The staff were always so discreet and good at protecting their members and guests from the media.

I was now meeting more and more people every day. Another good friend of mine was Joseph Al Khereji, Halcrow's agent in Saudi Arabia and a man of great wealth, with whom I spent a lot of time and who, like others before and after, helped to increase the size of my ever-growing portfolio of contacts. He threw the most fabulous parties all over the world, hiring singing stars like Julio Iglesias to entertain his guests. I met him through a business contact called Mohammed, himself the right-hand man to Ghazi Sultan, Saudi Arabia's Deputy Minister for Mineral Resources. My friendship with Joseph, though brief, all started when Mohammed called me out of the blue from Paris.

'Bienvenida,' he said, 'get ready, we are going on holiday. We are going to meet a friend of mine – his name is Joseph. Come to Nice quickly and his private jet will take us to Madrid, where he is giving a dinner party, and then we'll go on to Marbella the next day.'

I didn't need to be asked twice. It was a marvellous trip and Joseph turned out to be the most remarkable and wonderful man. He thought very highly of me and respected my business abilities, making it clear to his staff that they were to answer all my questions regarding his business and

Below: My mother, of whom my earliest recollections are that she was beautiful and elegant. She went to live in London when I was two years old, leaving me in the care of her mother.

Above: On a rare outing with my father, Francisco, a kind, gentle man of deep religious convictions.

Left: At 16, with my new hairstyle, when I too chose to head for London, that city of promise about which I had fantasized for so long.

Above: Me (right) with my maternal grandmother, Francisca, and my cousin Resita. My grandmother was the rock upon which my life was built.

Above: Seven Rivers Fête, 9 June 1990. With Vice Chairman of the Management Committee Dick Martins – and the wonderful hat. It was here that I made my début representing Sir Antony in his Colchester constituency. (Essex County Newspapers)

Opposite and above:
In my apartment in
St John's Wood,
London, into which Sir
Antony Buck, QC, MP,
moved with me.
In October 1989, six
months after we'd met,
Sir Antony and I had
become engaged to be
married.
(Rex Features)

Right: With Angela
and Michael in 1990
at the opening of their
new night club,
Valentino's in
Colchester.
(Essex County Newspapers)

Right: Christmas 1991: in Marrakesh with Sir Antony. We'd married in March 1990, and within a short time his possessiveness and jealousy began to show through.

Below: A festive Marrakesh – but, in December 1991, I finally asked Sir Antony for a divorce.

Above: In 1992, just before leaving for dinner at Sir Peter Harding's home. On public occasions Sir Antony's behaviour had became worse and he used to announce: 'My wife is having an affair with the Chief of Defence.'

Left: Air Chief Marshal Sir Peter Harding, whom I met in September 1990, at a dinner party in London hosted by the Indian High Commissioner.
(Rex Features)

Above: Lady Harding and Princess Helena Montafian, February 1991. Although Sir Peter was earning a six-figure salary, on social occasions his wife often used to complain that her husband was poorly paid.

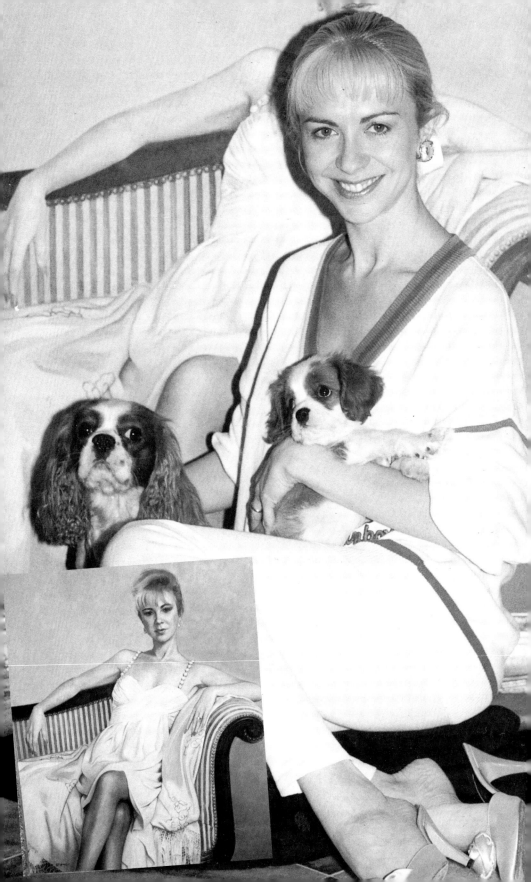

Below: My husband Count Nicholas Sokolow and I at the Royal Riviera in the South of France. Nicky had officially proposed to me at the Dorchester Club on 14 November 1993, exactly one year to the day after we met and three months after my divorce to Sir Antony was completed.
(Courtesy of the *News of the World*)

Left: Nicky, mushroom picking – his passion and my new hobby.

Overleaf: Facing difficulties with a smile.
(Rex Features)

Opposite: Caught without make-up! With Sasha as a puppy and Coco, June 1994. I used to walk my dogs with Sir Peter in London's Regent's Park.
(Photo courtesy *Sunday Express*)

Opposite inset: Sir Antony's wedding present in 1990: a portrait of me.

the running of his homes. I was very touched by that. Joseph had a brother who was blind but who had the truly remarkable gift of being able to identify colours by touch and who had a heart of gold. The parties Joseph threw at his villa and on his yacht were unbelievable. Along with Kano, he was one of the most dignified men I have ever met.

Mohammed and I flew with Ghazi Sultan to America to meet with officials from US Steel to discuss how Saudi Arabia might set up its own foundries with the help of the Americans. I went as Mohammed's personal assistant and was obliged to work hard, keeping track of meetings and taking down the details of the trip. For this I was handsomely rewarded, although I accepted the task mainly because of the opportunities that might arise from it. I was fascinated to watch these men dealing with American Government officials and it was a good learning experience. We flew first to Miami, where we stayed at the Hilton Fontainebleau Hotel, which has the most beautiful swimming-pool and cascades, and where we had a very enjoyable dinner with the Governor of Florida. There I also met and had a long and interesting talk with HRH Prince Sultan Ibn Abdulaziz, Saudi Arabia's Minister of Defence and Aviation.

Mohammed and I then flew the following day to Minneapolis and drove to Duluth, a mining community in the middle of what seemed to me like the Tundra, staying in a little motel amid all the cold and wetness. The area is rich in mineral resources and we visited US Steel's foundry there to see if it would be viable for the Saudi Arabian government to build similar plants for themselves. The Saudis wanted to learn from the Americans, planning in the future to buy their expertise rather than their products. They were doing this in many different areas, intending to become more self-sufficient so that they didn't have to keep importing everything from other countries. They were building nuclear, desalination and chemical plants as well as steel foundries. We were planning to go next to San Antonio in Texas, to look at the various reactors which produced atomic energy, but I didn't make that trip.

On the way back to Minneapolis from Duluth to catch the company plane, we were snowed in and I had to endure one of the worst trips of my life, being driven for hours along the desolate, icy roads. We had to reach Minneapolis because, as the airport there was international, they had installed subterranean heat dispersants under the tarmac so that the airport could function in all weathers. The process was developed by British Petroleum in Alaska for their pipelines and used most effectively at

Zurich Airport, to keep the planes operational in even the worst weather conditions.

After returning to London I decided that I needed a holiday. As I had never been to Greece before and because I had often heard about the beautiful islands, I flew out to Athens with a view to spending a couple of weeks relaxing and enjoying my independence. While there I bumped into a charming couple whom I knew from London. They were very hospitable and had a beautiful sailing boat on which I spent some time. I had taken a suite at the Astrid Hotel just outside Athens, going into the city to shop or lying around by the pool under a parasol when not on the yacht. Most days we would go out on the boat, cruising around the islands, stopping off at deserted beaches for barbecues and champagne, which would be set up for us by the crew, or dining in wonderful homes beside the sea. It was an idyllic break from London and I felt very refreshed on my return.

All the time that I had been travelling and spending time with my contacts and friends, I was awaiting my chance to start brokering deals for myself, in the same way as I had seen others do. I knew that I was building a network of people which would one day pay dividends, and I just needed a chance to start the wheels turning. I would read avidly such newspapers as the *Wall Street Journal* and the *Financial Times* in search of opportunities, although my first big deal turned out to come from a social contact.

In 1983 I became privy to the fact that a Middle Eastern government was inviting proposals for the construction of an airport. I called a contact of mine who I knew was both wealthy and had interests in engineering projects. I'd never worked with him before but I needed to draw on his expertise and experience. I briefed him by phone on the proposals being sought by the government concerned and said that I thought it might be a good idea if he had a meeting in London with the representative of a firm of consulting engineers whom I knew in the hope that the two of them would be able to come up with the necessary proposal to build the airport. He agreed, and having spoken to my contact at the engineering firm, I set up a lunch at the Connaught Hotel, which I knew to be very discreet.

The meeting was a great success and spawned further meetings between the two men, at which I was no longer present, having had my lawyers draw up a contract, which both of them signed, regarding my introductory fee. Ultimately they put together a proposal for the airport and the client accepted it. By introducing two of the parties concerned, I was able to claim a hefty six-figure commission based on the value of the whole contract. I was absolutely elated, as this was my first big deal, and to celebrate I treated myself to a luxurious and extravagant week in Milan from which the leading fashion houses there have never quite recovered.

Before long I was able to bring off yet another lucrative deal. A name and a contact number I had been given were those of Ahmed Gaddafi, Colonel Gaddafi's brother. At the time a trading embargo with Libya was in force and despite that country's being desperate to sell, it was impossible to buy any of its oil. I knew of a party in the Middle East whose government, not having a petrochemical industry of its own, was always keen to acquire oil while not being overconcerned about where it came from. Ahmed Gaddafi was staying at the Sheraton Park Tower in Knightsbridge and received a call from the interested party with whom I had put him in touch. I'd never met Ahmed and had only ever spoken to him on the phone. He was informed that I was the person he would be meeting and that it was to me that he would be talking. Despite being comparative young, I had learnt an enormous amount about the oil business and was fast becoming experienced in the arts of brokerage.

When I arrived at the hotel, Ahmed was not there, but had left a message for me to wait in his suite. When he finally turned up I took a strong dislike to him. He was tall and slim but seemed to me no more than an arrogant playboy and was blatantly dismissive of me because I was 'just a young woman who could know nothing about the oil business'. But I said nothing, while thinking that if I knew so little, how come he was still talking to me. I continued to absorb his empty rhetoric but refused to let him undermine my position, speaking calmly and with confidence, with rather frustrated him as he was being closely watched by his bodyguards and a Moroccan woman who was with him. Within a few weeks the deal was completed and I'd made yet another handsome sum in commission for my part in bringing the parties together. Now I really felt that I was beginning to make some progress as a businesswoman.

During this period I discovered the Villa d'Este, one of the most beautiful hotels in Europe, overlooking Lake Como in northern Italy. I went there with a man with whom I was to be for three years. George Karam was a Lebanese business contact who worked in Doha, the capital of Qatar, for a company called Gulf Services Consultants, which dealt in construction and engineering. Having cleared it with the head of the company, he made me his liaison officer in London. My job was to keep in touch with his clients, the main one being Charles Bonnington, a construction firm, coordinating the buying and selling of materials for different projects that they had undertaken in the Middle East. George put me on a good six-figure salary, which I felt I could command at that stage, but the work was hard and I certainly had to earn it.

I had met George at a diplomatic reception in London and first we became good friends and then he fell in love with me, which had been my intention all along. He was a charming man and introduced me to his family, ringing me regularly not only to liaise with me about the work I was doing for him but also because he cared for me deeply and was concerned about my welfare. The Villa d'Este is a superb classical building and a wonderful hotel which at the time was full of old-world charm and decadence, but boasted one of the finest international clienteles in the world. In the summer season they would serve wonderful buffets, although this is not something I like ordinarily. I find it undignified to have to queue up for food and I always ask a waiter to go and make a choice on my behalf. I think it is more elegant. After dinner we would go out on the terrace overlooking the lake and dance to live music with the lights reflecting on the calm waters below. During the days we would take a boat across the lake to enjoy lunch at other hotels or to visit the lovely market in the nearby village of Cernobbio. I was having the most wonderful time.

George became totally besotted by me, telling me he wanted to leave his wife and marry me. He even introduced me to his eleven-year-old son, a lovely boy with the most wonderful manners, who was at Sherborne School in Dorset, and to his aunt, who lived in an apartment opposite Kano's house in Farm Street. The aunt liked me and was a terribly elegant woman with two gorgeous sons. 'I would be so proud,' she told me, 'if one of my sons had a wife like you.' I think that it was one of the nicest things anyone had ever said to me.

Eventually, after three years of being with George, I was getting a little bored and hurt him rather badly when at last I met the boss of the whole company. He was a man called Ahmed, whom George had taken me to meet in Monte Carlo. Ahmed had a yacht in the harbour and a beautiful Aston-Martin Lagonda. He was completely bowled over by me and within days of our meeting he began to lavish gifts on me, with promises of even more. He desperately wanted to have an affair with me and seemed to have a good deal more to offer than George. Sticking firmly to my philosophy, I told George what had happened and asked him how he felt about it. 'I feel heartbroken,' he said, and I noticed that he was crying, 'because I love you, Bienvenida. But I know that I must put my feelings aside and allow you to be with Ahmed because he is my employer.' This, I thought, was extremely convenient.

Of course, I had to give up my job as liaison officer but that didn't bother me because there were bigger stakes to play for. I did feel a bit sorry for George, but by that time I was more practical than most men and invariably less emotionally attached, if at all. I did understand that, rather like the incident with Ali and Kano, I was a sort of gift from George to his boss, and that suited me perfectly. If this delightful Middle Eastern tradition of stepping down in favour of the more senior men was to go on, however, I was worried that eventually I would reach whoever the top man was and then have nowhere to go; or maybe when that happened you went down to the bottom and started all over again – a concept I found extremely amusing. But George was full of insecurities and I had discovered that once men started to talk about leaving their families, it is time to end the relationship. I certainly didn't want to get married and having a man constantly troubled by his conscience is a bore. If and when that happened I bestowed upon them a memorable night and would then say goodbye. People don't realize that I have kept far more families together than I have ever broken up.

Ahmed and I were to enjoy a fun relationship and remain friends for some time.

6

Toys and Texas

ano and I would meet from time to time in London at places like Annabel's or Les Ambassadeurs. We would return to the mansion in Farm Street, where, if I felt it was in my interests, I would stay. Kano had a very loyal English butler who would discreetly look after me in the morning by preparing breakfast and then very politely order a cab and see me out of the door. You have to be very careful of other people's staff, for their loyalties will always be to those who are paying their salaries. Never make the mistake of speaking too intimately with someone's driver, household staff or security people because they will almost certainly report straight back to their employers. When you are being driven by a silent and unobtrusive chauffeur, his eyes fixed on the road and apparently concentrating on his driving, it is all too easy to forget that he is there and talk idly and indiscreetly in the back, perhaps with a girlfriend. Anyone who hears private conversations in this way is likely to pass them on and if you are hoping to build a good network of contacts it is unwise to make such mistakes.

Les Ambassadeurs, at the bottom of Park Lane, was a very elegant club with a beautiful conservatory. The food was exquisite, the service faultless and the staff charming and discreet. They had been very happy to have me as a member because I maintained the club's high standards, attended frequently and was always accompanied by highly suitable guests. I have always made a point of being polite, considerate and charming to staff in any hotel, private residence, or restaurant that I visit, and when it is appropriate I can be very generous. Many women don't realize how important femininity and good manners are in gaining respect from the people around you. If you treat them as if they are inferiors, ordering them around without so much as a "please" or "thank you" and are mean as well, they will be very reluctant to do anything for you in return. But if they know that you respect them and their position, you will find that they will happily go out of their way to accommodate and look after you. Should a situation arise in a restaurant or hotel where there is cause to complain, it ought to be done with the minimum of fuss, discreetly and with firm dignity, out of earshot of any other guests.

Gradually I lost touch with Kano but over the years I would occasionally see him at Les Ambassadeurs. He had grown stooped and hunched, suddenly seemed much older, and apparently had difficulty in walking. I was shocked to see in what a short time a man can change. A little rule that I have is that I never believe in making a fuss when I see someone I know across a room. I think it extremely vulgar to go over and plant flamboyant kisses on the cheeks, as so many women do. I acknowledge the person with a smile and a gentle nod of the head, having no wish to embarrass or compromise them in front of who ever they are with.

My friendships and business deals with Middle Eastern men had taught me much about the ways in which they conduct business. You need a lot of patience to succeed in opening commercial avenues in that part of the world because everyone likes to give the impression of being very laid-back and in no hurry to achieve results. They do not believe in rushing a deal. They prefer, like the Orientals, to take time to get to know the people with whom they are dealing, to build relationships of mutual trust before deciding to commit themselves to a course of action. Some Western business people find this process very tedious and time-consuming, preferring to storm in and deal first, letting the lawyers argue and wrangle about the details later. In my experience the Western approach is based on greed as well as a desire for instant personal gain. Consequently it often causes tremendous antagonism and bad feeling between people who should be concentrating on building long-term partnerships and not short-term sacrifices.

At that time all the Middle Eastern economies were flourishing as a result of the great boom in oil and the money that this generated. Many of the Arabs who turned up in London were like children suddenly let loose in a toyshop, finding themselves able to buy anything they wanted. Their behaviour made many in London secretly despise them while remaining very happy to take their money. But these Arabs were very different from the men that I knew and was mixing with socially and professionally. The men I met were from established families that were used to having money and influence, most of which had been wealthy for many generations. All the important trading families in the Middle East were written about in a book called *The Merchants*, published in the eighties. I didn't read it until later and was surprised to discover just how powerful and deep-rooted my friends were. Their influence stretched much further then I had ever imagined.

During this time I was still putting a lot of thought into what it was that men find attractive in women. Wishing as I did to portray the image of the 'perfect' woman and to provide whatever it was that they were looking for, it was a subject upon which I reflected a good deal. I suspect that, aside from all the intangibles, one of the most important qualities in a woman is to be vivacious and outgoing all the time, not embittered and unhappy but always smiling and pleasant like a carefree young girl. No man wants to be burdened with the problems of a woman. He wants to be enchanted, entertained, distracted, intrigued and excited. Even if I was feeling unwell or unhappy about something, I would always make an effort to be refreshing, youthful and positive on the outside whenever I was in company.

Of course, intimacy played an important part as far as men were concerned but I had realized that the sex appeal needed to interest a man has nothing to do with the vulgarity of a big cleavage, or even great physical beauty – it is all far more subtle than that. Real beauty comes from within and achieving it is very hard work indeed, requiring time, intelligence and sufficient motivation in the first place. I have learnt many lessons, some unpleasant, from my experiences in life, but I have not allowed them to make me bitter or jealous because I know that if that were to happen I would be finished, no longer interesting or fun to be with and no longer a distraction from the rest of life's ugly pageant.

There are many different skills which can easily be acquired or learnt but which most women never bother about, happy to leave it to the men in their lives. I wanted, for example, to learn all about fine wines and cognacs so that I could choose on behalf of guests at dinner parties. I also wanted to be able to choose the men's cigars for them, so I bought a book on the subject, read it and then used to go to Davidoff to talk to the staff in order to learn more. In the finer things of life, I never wanted to feel it any way inferior to any man.

On the whole, I get on much better with men than women. I have so frequently been disappointed with the way women behave towards one another. They often seem to simply take advantage of others and have no idea how to either conduct or benefit from a good friendship. They seem to be distracted by an envy which blinds them to the opportunities which sometimes present themselves. I am not advocating for one moment that friendships ought to be looked upon only with opportunistic intent. They can be very rewarding in terms of comfort, the source of great hilarity and fun and can form the basis of a healthy and normal emotional support system. I have lost count of the number of women over the years who have complained to me that I am 'so lucky', not realizing how hard I have had to work to earn that luck or that, if they so chose, they could do exactly the same thing with a little motivation and self-confidence.

It is often surprising which of one's casual acquaintances grow to become one's closest friends. I met Michael George at a reception given by Crédit Suisse Bank in 1980 to say goodbye to a departing manager and welcome his replacement. We were both clients of the bank and our first encounter was quite unintentional. Michael was an Iraqi who lived in St John's Wood. He was in his early forties but had never married, having devoted all his energies to looking after his large and demanding family. He was a very kind, charming and intelligent man, well dressed and an engineer by training, which was probably one of the reasons why I found it so easy to talk to him at the reception. He had a rugged and weathered face and his hair was flecked with grey. He took me home that evening as it was around the corner from where he lived and promptly called me the next day.

We became close friends, but later a close intimacy developed. The two of us often travelled to Geneva together when either he or I went over for banking reasons or when he had to meet one of his business partners who lived there. The trips were anything but arduous, just overseeing of investments and a few meetings, leaving us free to spend most of our time enjoying the pleasures of the beautiful city. The family's wealth derived mainly from engineering contracts with the Iraqi government but they also had business connections with Mercedes-Benz and other trading interests. There were also numerous factories in Iraq and the family had the Rolex franchise for that area of the world.

In some senses Michael was a little unsophisticated, with rather simple tastes, and although, sadly, he never asked me to marry him, he was the only man up to that time that I had seriously considered suitable to be my husband. He did tell me that he would marry me if he could but that he still had a permanent responsibility to his family and was never really likely to become involved in marriage unless he could devote himself to it completely. I thought that this was probably only partially true and because it is in my nature to be suspicious of all men, no matter how honourable they appear to be, I suspected that either Michael was secretly engaged to someone else or he was seeing other women and didn't want to give up that sort of lifestyle. I had no proof of any of this but, as far as I was concerned, my opinions then or ever required neither confirmation nor justification. (I was to use this convenient attitude in never acknowledging fault on those occasions when I was proved wrong.)

But there was another reason for not marrying which Michael never disclosed to me even though to have done so would have eliminated the unpleasantness that developed later on. He had been diagnosed as having lymphatic cancer and had only a few years to live. Michael was a lovely man and during the four years we were together he was very generous and we shared a lot of good times. Towards the end of his life, he became increasingly sick and consequently aggressive towards me, for some reason feeling either unwilling or unable to share with me the burden of his deteriorating condition. Over a period of weeks his generosity and affection for me began to wane and he also became possessive, which is a trait I have never liked in men when it is not justified. I had given him no reason to revise his attitude towards me and couldn't understand why these changes were happening.

Often Michael would be in bed in his flat when I visited and he would say it was because he had a bad back, but I could see that he was losing weight and nothing seemed to make any sense. I also failed to understand why, if he was in such discomfort and spending so much time in bed, he was not going either to a clinic in Switzerland or allowing himself to be attended by a doctor. Even though I was not privy to the depressing truth about his condition, I definitely felt that there was something seriously wrong as the atmosphere surrounding him seemed permanently laden with doom. I knew that something serious was being hidden from me but, unable to find out what it was, I became angry at his behaviour and ended up by saying some cruel and regrettable things which I would never have dreamt of saying if I had know the truth of the situation. We had been together for so long, and I regretted never being able to take back those unkind things before he passed away.

In my frustration, and acting in an unusually callous fashion, I told him bluntly that if he was not prepared to marry me as he had occasionally intimated he might, I was going to leave him for someone else. I did not want to waste my time with him if he was not going to commit himself to me and I still had to consider my own security and long-term financial future. Although there was a degree of acrimony as a result of our parting in such a fashion, the doors were still open as far as I was concerned. However, it meant that I now felt free to pursue other avenues for increasing my financial goals.

Around this time I was introduced to a man called Dr Ali Naghavi at a dinner party. He was a heart surgeon who had moved from Iran to Los Angeles and used to come to London on business as he had a partnership with Beecham Pharmaceuticals. Ali was an amazingly charming man and treated me beautifully. As with Michael, our affair started slowly and it was not until we had taken the time to get to know each other that we became physically involved. The very first evening that we ever went out to dinner together he arranged for me to receive a bouquet of red roses at the table and when I left the restaurant I carried them in my arms. It felt wonderful. Ali was married, however, and had an Iranian wife and three grown-up children in California, although he told me that the marriage was no longer happy and that he was spending less and less time at home.

After leaving London he was in touch with me almost every day. He also had a financial set-up in Switzerland as he was moving his money out of Iran before the deposition of the Shah, and from time to time he would rendezvous with me in Geneva. He would always meet me at the airport with a bouquet of orchids and, as many had done before and a few after, he valued me as a friend, appreciated me as a woman and was prepared to invest in me for the support, comfort and companionship I was happy to offer in return. He was tall and handsome, around fifty years old with blue eyes and a disarming and gentle manner. When he came to London he used to stay at the Ritz as he felt it was more private than the Grosvenor House, and he always took two suites so that I could change in privacy before dinner. Even though I had my beautiful apartment in St John's Wood and had been through a series of apartments, on each of which I had made a considerable profit, it was fun to stay in the hotel.

By this time Noel and I had become no more than friends, which suited us both very well, and although I had never allowed any opportunities to bypass me when we had been more closely involved, I felt much happier and much more at liberty to pursue my own quest for independence. I was also still in touch with Michael, our relationship having become one of friendship, for I was still very concerned about his health.

Ali and I decided a few months after we met to spend Christmas together in New York. I suggested taking Concorde, which we did, and we stayed in an apartment at the Waldorf Towers. Christmas is a wonderful time of year in New York, but so cold outside that the good department stores offer their clients hot coffee and cookies. The first few days were idyllic and I can safely say that for the two years we were together he treated me as if I were the most precious piece of porcelain. He said that he wanted to spend the rest of his life with me. I would take care of his needs in every way I could, just as I would take care of any of the men with whom I chose to spend time. I knew, for instance, that he always liked his butter cold and I would order ice cubes in advance for the butter dishes placed on the tables of restaurants or at breakfast. I would always check the table before we went down for dinner to ensure that everything was the way he liked it.

Two days before Christmas we walked down Madison Avenue to Régine's nightclub. It was an incredibly clear, icily cold evening. When we returned to the apartment in the hotel he said, 'I am not going to sleep next to you tonight because I am feeling a little unwell.' He then spent the night in the other bed and on the morning of Christmas Eve he told me that he thought there was something wrong with his heart. 'Please,' he said, 'call the doctor.'

The hotel doctor brought a portable electrocardiograph and established that Ali's heartbeat was very irregular. They did some blood tests and then called for an ambulance. I had to gain access to his safety deposit box in the hotel, and so told the staff that I was his wife in order to get out his medical card and follow the necessary instructions.

'I give you power of attorney,' Ali told me as the hotel security people came in to seal the room. 'There are about six thousand pounds in Swiss francs in the hotel safe. Take that and get yourself back to London.' I didn't take the money as I did not think that it was a dignified thing to do. I was in the ambulance with him as we bumped and crashed along the uneven Manhattan roads with the siren wailing, heading for the Lennox Hill Hospital. It felt like the longest journey of my life. In the hospital, the doctors were crowding round him and I could tell from the way they were talking that he was having a massive heart attack. I was totally hysterical, crying my eyes out at the thought of losing him. Luckily, he had always spoken very highly of me to his sister, Mona, who lived in Detroit. I contacted her and she said that she would fly in on the next available plane.

By now I was in such a state that the doctors told me they didn't want me around. They sent me back to the hotel, where I sat up waiting until Mona arrived at about one-thirty in the morning and I was then able to hand over the power of attorney to her. I booked a seat on Concorde as the arrival of Ali's wife from Los Angeles was imminent and packed my cases in a state of complete shock and exhaustion. I also took the time to call Michael in London, as I had been doing, but this time it was not to find out how he was but to tell him of the situation. I desperately needed someone to be there for me when I arrived, someone on whom I could lean because, although I was very fond of Ali rather than in love with him, I found the prospect of losing him quite hard to face.

Before leaving for the airport I went downstairs at the Waldorf Towers to get a coffee and I noticed a man watching me across the restaurant. That is quite normal, but at that moment I felt self-conscious because of the state I was in, knowing I looked dreadful. The same man arrived in the Concorde lounge later, and came over to ask if I was all right. I was so distraught and overcome that I broke one of my golden rules and, desperate to pour out my troubles, opened up to him and told him the whole story about Ali. He apologized for staring at me in the hotel restaurant but said that I looked like someone in dire need of help and support. It transpired in time that he was the insurance broker for British Airways with special responsibility for the fleet of fourteen Concorde aircraft and carried some weight within the company. He managed to hold up the plane for a few minutes while I made a final call to the hospital and then arranged for me to sit in the cabin for take-off, to distract me from my worries. The pilot was Captain John Cook, whom I'd met before, so it was a friendly flight. And on our return to London my white knight invited me out to dinner to keep my spirits up.

When we arrived at Heathrow, Michael was waiting for me and I broke down, crying uncontrollably. He was very supportive and understanding but I was totally distraught, still angry with him for hiding unknown things from me and although I'd asked him to be there when I arrived, I said some things a few days later which I rather regretted afterwards. 'If it were not,' I said harshly, 'for the fact that Ali had had a heart attack, I wouldn't be here, so don't assume I am here because I want to be with you.' I spent some time with him over the Christmas period and nothing more was said about my rather unprovoked remarks. However, Michael was very gaunt and most of the time remained very subdued and quiet, talking less and less. I did try to persuade him to take a trip with me to lift his spirits, but he was too weak.

In January, still upset over Ali and more and more concerned that Michael was deteriorating, I went to see my mother. I hadn't seen her for a long time although she was still receiving the benefits of my generosity. This was probably not the wisest thing to do at the time but I was looking for some sympathy and support and, since she knew full well the source of the money from which she was ultimately benefiting, I did expect her to at least hear me out and offer me her shoulder. I was still desperate for the two of us to mend our differences and I felt that if I went to her as a daughter in need of some maternal support, she might respond to my needs. I related the tales of Ali and Michael. 'It is you that are driving these men to their graves,' she said. 'It is all your fault.' Her words once again hurt me deeply and I went home feeling worse than I had for a long time.

After two weeks Ali left hospital and flew home to Los Angeles. The doctors told him to stop drinking, which he was not prepared to do. Like so many doctors, he was being neglectful of his own health. When he next came to England I took him to see a well-known cardiologist in Harley Street as he wanted to know as much as possible about the options open to him. We went to see her after her normal consulting hours and she spent the evening with Ali, administering a local anaesthetic and then using angioplasty, which was then still very new and involved putting the finest fibre-optic cable in through a vein in his upper arm to see what was going on in his heart. She very sweetly refused to charge him because he was a fellow professional, which I thought was a wonderfully noble gesture. I was very worried about Ali and disapproved of his drinking but didn't want to nag him. He was with me because it made him happy and if I started to interfere like a wife, pestering him and become a bore, I would probably end up the loser.

Ali was always touched that I had not taken the Swiss francs which he had offered me when he was in hospital in New York, but I was always careful not to make men I was with feel that I would ever take advantage of them in a way that was insulting or displayed greed or vulgarity. I had once been in Paris with George Karam's boss, Ahmed. I didn't like the hotel in which we were staying, the Grand, and so we changed to the Crillon. Somewhere in the course of the move I lost the pochette containing all the jewels which I had brought with me. Although I told Ahmed what had happened, I didn't make a fuss about it because I was concerned that he might think I was trying to induce him into replacing them. It was the most expensive weekend of my life.

Michael was finally admitted to the London Clinic about two months after Ali's heart attack in New York, telling me he was going in for his back problems. He looked a little thin but not too bad. There were still one or two things that didn't add up but I put them to the back of my mind. His family were spending more and more time with him, so I couldn't really be there as much as I would have liked, which I found very galling and didn't understand. Dr Rau, who was Michael's GP and later became my doctor as well, used to come and sit with him every morning but I still could not work out why Michael refused to come abroad somewhere with me in order to recover. I realized that I was getting nowhere and decided that if my presence was not welcome, as it apparently wasn't, I might as well get on with my own life and not allow Michael's condition to distract me from all the things I still wanted to achieve.

I had met Amparo through my mother, during one of my visits to Spain and she had become a kind and loyal friend to me. She had just given birth to a little girl whose name, Chanel, I had been allowed to choose. Amparo had invited me to be the godmother and so I went to Valencia to attend the christening.

While I was there I decided to see my father. Although I had been back to Valencia on an earlier occasion, it was when I still felt that there was some veracity to my mother's opinions and stories about my father. However, I no longer believed anything she said, and finally chose to meet up with him against her express wishes. It was a difficult decision and I was filled with anxiety about how I would react after twenty years. Naturally I wanted to see if there was anything I could do to help him and compensate for having chosen to ignore his existence for so long.

My previous visits to the town of my birth had resulted in my buying an apartment, which I still had though it was not furnished or decorated. On my first visit to Valencia I had not wanted to stay with my mother and her boyfriend Paul in the old apartment where, as a little girl, I had lived with my grandmother, and so had spent two weeks in a hotel. Later I had wanted to return there for another summer break but when I asked my mother whether I could stay in her flat, the refusal had prompted me to purchase my own. I was now seriously thinking about offering it to my father, scant recompense though it was, for not having been in touch for so many years. I was staying in the same hotel as before, the Astoria, and straight after arriving went off in search of him wearing little jewellery and dressed in an elegant but simple outfit. I went back to the little house where I had been born and spent the first six years of my life. It looked so tiny and shabby, hidden away in the backstreet, but other than seeming smaller than I remembered, everything was exactly the same. Unable to elicit any response from the house and workshop, which were completely shuttered, I went to the shop next door to ask them if they knew of my father's whereabouts.

'Hola, are you Mari-Bienve?' asked the old woman, using a shortening of my name that I hadn't heard in years. 'Yes,' I replied, unable to believe that someone would recognize me after twenty years, then asked where I might find my father. She told me what a lovely man Francisco was and how much everyone in the community liked and respected him. I was already beginning to feel emotional, and having spent years listening to my mother denigrating the poor man, to hear this old shopkeeper speaking so highly of him was making things much worse. She went on to explain that at that time of the day he would most probably be in the bar around the corner, playing cards. I made my way to the place she described, one of the countless working men's bars which you find in every Spanish town and village.

As I approached I could see through the window a group of men sitting on simple wooden chairs round a table. They had glasses of rough

Spanish wine and coffee cups beside them and were holding their cards firmly, intent on their game. They were all talking at once except for my father, who was sitting silently staring at his cards, seemingly miles away. He had lost nothing of the dignity which I had always ascribed to him, but he was older, a little more gaunt and frail. He glanced up as I came through the door but then looked away, not because I had changed so much but because mine was probably the last face in the world that he'd been expecting to see. He slowly looked round again and as I stood there completely numb a frown crossed his face, followed by a huge smile. Tears came into his eyes and he stood up and came over to me and we embraced warmly.

I was less overcome than he was, not because the poignancy of the moment was lost on me but simply because I have never been the kind of person who is able to outwardly display strong emotion. His voice was just as I remembered, quiet and dignified. We left the bar and went for a walk through the streets. It was difficult if not impossible to catch up on all the news of our separate lives but he told me about himself and about the quiet life he now led and I simply told him that I was busy and happy living in London.

Then I gave him some money and promised to come back soon. I also told him that, as he didn't have a telephone in the house, he should stay in touch with Amparo and let me know if he needed anything but that I was only in Valencia for one more day in order to attend Chanel's christening. I could see that there was no point in offering him the flat at that stage as he was obviously quite happy in the little house where he had always lived. Nevertheless, having re-established contact, I was determined to help him in any way I could from now on.

When I returned to London, being the glutton for punishment that I must have been, I went to see my mother. This strange hold that she seemed to have over me and which kept me going back to her again and again despite the way she treated me, was probably no more than a variation on the pull that all parents, the world over, exert on their children. I still wanted her approval, I still wanted to forge some sort of bond with her and I seemed determined to persevere with my efforts. It didn't seem to matter to me that the abuse was going to continue no matter what.

My mother knew that I had bought a flat in Valencia and started asking me about it. She told me that her flat, the one I knew from my childhood and which she refused to let me use, was making her unhappy as a result of the memories it contained and that the neighbours were constantly interfering with her privacy. My response was to offer her the use of mine for the duration of any visits she might make in the future. But that wasn't enough.

'I must have it,' she told me.

'You're welcome to use it any time you like,' I assured her.

'That's not good enough,' she insisted, 'I need the security of knowing that it is mine.'

How I was able to be so intolerant and unforgiving of ill-treatment from men and yet unable to resist the pressures my mother subjected me to, I simply do not know. Of course, I fell for her story about her apartment in Valencia and went to a solicitor to make the necessary arrangements. A few days after the paperwork had been completed and the deal finalized, the solicitor rang to tell me my mother had issued him with instructions to sell the flat. I rang her to find out what was happening.

'How could you give me something which I can't afford to look after?' she complained and I then realized that all she had wanted was the money and that the stories about her apartment were designed to make me act as I did. However, despite my deciding that this really was the last straw, it wasn't.

The next time I rang to find out how Michael was his nephew, Hakim, told me that he had died of lymphatic cancer. Suddenly I understood his behaviour over the previous months and I was most terribly hurt that he had felt unable to tell me. But as well as being saddened by his death, I felt very guilty for having spoken the way I had. If only I had known the truth, I would not have gone to New York and would never have been so aggressive in trying to get him to marry me. I now wished earnestly that I had made his last few months more pleasant and realized I would never be able to say sorry, thank you or goodbye. I was very sad, very angry at myself and consequently became very depressed. In time the pain was to pass and all the more so when I learnt that some of the suspicions that I'd had about Michael were true. Apparently he had been secretly engaged to another woman as well as having the odd girlfriend apart from me. But it hadn't stopped him being very warm and generous to me.

Hakim was a charming young student whom I had met briefly at Michael's flat once before. Aside from Dr Rau, he was the only person who had known the truth about his uncle's illness and when Michael finally died it was Hakim who comforted me, while the rest of his family acted as if I didn't exist. I suppose they were probably terrified that someone from outside the family might get hold of some of Michael's money. Hakim, who was only a year older than me, was obliged to take control of the family's assets but his forte lay in being a genius at computer science rather than a financial expert. He was in any case still too young to undertake the responsibility for, or even understand, the pitfalls and problems associated with managing the family's substantial business concerns.

'It was my uncle's wish that I should look after you and I want you to know that you can rely on me if there is ever anything you need,' he told me. It was a promise which he has kept to this day. We became very good friends and I would like to feel that over the years, in return for all his loyalty and kindness, I have been able to offer him a little assistance and guidance in the ways of the world, for he had, and still has in fact, a tendency to be a little complacent and negligent with his appearance. I was able to help him to choose clothes and assist in his becoming a little more sophisticated. Also, I showed him how to enjoy the new lifestyle which had been thrust upon him. We would go to Geneva together, where Michael held all his bank accounts, and usually took a suite at the Noga Hilton, on the banks of the lake, one of the most beautiful new hotels of the time. Sometimes when I went to Geneva on my own later, I would stay at the Beau Rivage, a smaller, more traditional hotel rather like the Connaught in London, but I still prefer the Noga with its high technology and clean, modern lines. Hakim is one of the most genuine and kind people I have ever known and still remains a very good friend. He has never hurt or lied to me and if he has a fault it is that he is too open, honest and trusting.

Soon after Michael's death I received the sad news that my father had also died. I was at my apartment at the time, having dinner with Hakim, when the call came from Amparo in Spain and I was utterly devastated. He had died alone in that little house, of a heart attack, only four months after my visit. Once again I had missed my chance to help somebody whom I ought to have been there for and there was nothing I could do about it. I became even more depressed and it was Hakim who did his level best to try to cheer me up.

One day, when we were walking in the Rue du Rhône in Geneva, looking in the windows of the jewellery shops, he said, 'I would like to buy you a present, Bienvenida. What would make you happy?' I laughed and said that, rather than jewellery, I would prefer to have a Ferrari. Hakim just nodded and said, 'OK, we'll buy it when we get back to London.'

As soon as we returned we went straight to H.R. Owen's showrooms in South Kensington and were shown a navy-blue 328 GTS. The salesman took me out for a test drive and, having decided that I couldn't possibly live a moment longer without this beautiful vehicle, I went back to Hakim, who quietly gave me the money.

In the three months before Michael died, when I felt that our relationship was not going anywhere, I had started flying out to Los Angeles to be with Ali as his doctors didn't like him taking long trips to London. I would stay at the Beverly Wilshire, taking Concorde as far as New York or Washington, staying overnight to relax, and then fly on to Los Angeles in the morning. I found the city fascinating, with its beautiful modern buildings and open design, particularly the area where I stayed around Rodeo Drive with all its glittering shops. LA had the sort of weather I liked, the colourful parties, great shops and wonderful food.

Ali was very proud to be seen with me, and the early trips were a great success. I had got to know his sister and his son and so I was not hidden away from his family. However, his behaviour became gradually meaner over the months. I think that people who live through an experience that brings them close to death change in many ways. I noticed that his personality had begun to alter for the worse, as had Michael's: slowly he became more selfish and less caring, as well as possessive. He also started making all kinds of promises and then not keeping them and I don't like men who promise things and then don't honour their word.

As I used never to continue relationships with men who didn't treat me with complete respect and sincerity, I decided to call it a day with Ali. Although I stopped seeing him for good, we did stay in touch and he continued to send me a bouquet of beautiful yellow tea roses every Christmas until he died two years later, to thank me for having helped save his life in New York.

One of the people Ali had introduced to me through an Iranian friend of his in the arms business was an American called Alex Holland. Alex used to buy surplus military equipment which the American government had left in Vietnam and which they wanted to get rid of cheaply rather than having to pay to ship it back to the States. Alex was constantly looking for buyers and Ali knew that I had many contacts around the world, so he arranged that we should get together in London. As a result, I met Alex at the Intercontinental Hotel at Hyde Park Corner.

Third World countries are always on the look-out for surplus military equipment from foreign governments, especially after a big war, when supplies outstrip demand and prices are consequently low. I had it in mind to introduce Alex to a third party of whom I had learnt and with whom I had become quite friendly. The potential buyer was staying in San Diego, just down the coast from Alex's home in the prestigious Holmby Hills area of Los Angeles. So it was arranged that I would fly out to the West Coast at Christmas time and spend the holiday with Alex and his teenage son at his impressive house overlooking a lake. Then we would drive down together to San Diego to meet my contact.

Alex was divorced, good-looking but a little overweight and very keen to impress me with the fact that he had purchased a penthouse in LA worth some ridiculous amount of money, where he said we could live together. He was full of grand schemes and plans but I began to suspect that not many of them, if any at all, were likely to come to fruition. He asked me to marry him but I felt that it would be unwise to ally myself to him too closely because of the questionable nature of his future. I did think, however, that we stood a good chance with the armaments deal and so I said nothing about misgivings. I got on very well with his son, John, who had reached a very confusing age and went on calling me from the States for some time after I returned to London, asking for advice on how to cope with his parents, which I thought rather touching.

I had an address and telephone number for my contact in San Diego. We called him and arranged a meeting, giving him an idea of what we had available to sell in terms of hardware. We then drove down the freeway to the very simple house where he was living with his wife and children. He was a government official from an Asian country, keeping a very low profile while in the USA. I was to be paid twenty percent commission on the deal and decided that because Alex had too much to lose by double-crossing me he would probably pay up if it went through. As it turned out, the official bought a large volume of military equipment and Alex paid me my share without complaint. I dare say he imagined that I would be in a position to arrange other such lucrative deals for him in the future if he treated me correctly and honestly.

A complication that can occur with an arms deal when you are selling to a blacklisted foreign country is that you need an 'end user's certificate' approved by the American, British or French governments, depending on which of these owns or is making the goods. To get that certificate you have to say that the arms are going somewhere like Taiwan, where there is no arms embargo. Once in Taiwan, the equipment can then be resold to a third party who would not have been able to acquire the goods through normal channels. The paperwork, however, was not a problem. As usual, I had simply been required to bring two sides together so that they could deal.

My life over the previous ten years had been fairly hectic, although very successful. However, the deaths of my father and Michael so close to each other had left me sad and depressed and I seemed to have become tired of London. My private life had been tumultuous and the pressures taxing. I didn't feel that I had the time or space to take stock and think about what I really wanted to achieve next. I had achieved much more than I had any right to expect and was now fully financially independent. For ten years I had pursued my ambitions tenaciously and without ceasing, but the result was that whereas it had been so easy to let the men in my life become emotionally attached to me, what I wanted now was to dispense with them. But since I didn't want to sever ties completely, this was going to take a considerable amount of tact and diplomacy. It was nice to know how they felt about me and that they wanted me in their lives, but I felt that perhaps I had been a little too successful and needed a break.

Also, I was still determined to become more rounded as a woman and achieve further successes. I knew that I ought to push myself even further and find a new challenge. As Zola's heroine Nana says, 'I was conscious of a void in my existence, a gap which made me yawn.' I became moody and no longer wanted to lead the frivolous life I had known thus far. I wanted to be more settled and to have more direction, but I wasn't really sure how to achieve that. I suddenly found that my desire to go out with my friends had gone. One of Kano's brothers called me one night at around twelve-thirty and invited me to a party, but whereas I would have said yes unhesitatingly in my earlier days, I suddenly heard myself saying no. I felt it was time to move on.

'You can do anything you like,' Hakim told me when I confided in him. 'Take a university course or travel, whatever you want.'

In the end I decided to go to Texas. I was feeling tired of London with its cold winters and the sad associations with the hurt I felt after Michael's death. I enrolled for a course in fashion design and merchandising, thinking that I might open a boutique in Dallas. A dear friend of mine, Philip Sommerville, the famous milliner, used to supply a boutique in Dallas and the owner recommended a course at Miss Wade's Fashion Merchandising College, in Dallas's Apparel Mart, as being the best in the USA. Having no other contacts in Texas, I needed to find a way to introduce myself to the city of Dallas on my own terms and in my own inimitable way. I called Merrill Lynch, the merchant bank in New York, and asked to speak to the department which dealt with real estate. Having been put through to the appropriate person in Texas, I explained that I was acting as an independent purchaser from London with over three million dollars to invest and was looking to buy a property in Dallas. I asked if they were in a position to recommend someone who could look into my request on my arrival in Texas. At that stage I wasn't sure whether I would actually be buying or not, but I certainly wanted to be shown around the right types of property.

Merrill Lynch put me in touch with a realtor in Texas, whom I called to explain my position. A tall, elegant and professional woman, she was kind enough to meet me at the airport and show me the best areas in Dallas.

'Where,' I asked her, 'could I spend a few months while I am looking around all these places, analysing the market conditions and making a decision?'

She showed me where she would live were she in my position: the Shelton, a beautiful apartment block in Highland Park Village, away from downtown Dallas. I followed her advice and arranged to rent an apartment there. It was an area full of beautiful houses with immaculate lawns and swimming pools. While I was waiting for the agreement to be sorted out, I stayed for two weeks at one of the best hotels, the Mansion, on Turtle Creek. It is certainly the best hotel in Texas, if not in the world: a Texas-style ranch owned by Caroline Hunt, one of the wealthiest women in America and sister of Bunker Hunt, the American billionaire, whom I was to meet, a man notorious for having tried to corner the silver market. I liked Caroline a lot. She was a woman of great energy despite being in her sixties and enjoyed a very active social life. The first night that I walked into the hotel's restaurant the head waiter sat me at a table next to one where Mark Thatcher and the woman he was courting to be his future wife were sitting. He seemed a very unimpressive man.

The views from the apartment at the Shelton were wonderful and I would wake up every morning to a spectacular sunrise. Even though I was there to have a break, I still didn't want to waste a single moment of the day. While I had been studying elocution with Professor de Campanet in London, I had recorded our classes and had brought some of the tapes with me to Dallas. As I got myself ready in the morning I would play them in order to practise the exercises she had taught me. I wanted to avoid developing even the slightest American accent and to ensure that I continued to speak good English.

I would leave for 'Miss Wade's school', as the college was known, at seven-thirty in the morning, working until one o'clock, learning about the history of fashion, the industrial and business processes involved as well as practical skills like how to cut patterns. It was a huge college, forming part of an impressive modern marketing complex. Miss Wade was a tall woman in her fifties, always well presented, and I suspected that she had once been a model. Although I really wanted to study the business aspects, it was also important to understand everything else associated with the fashion industry, to be able to appreciate fine fabrics, their properties and their potential.

At one o'clock almost every day I would go to Highland Park for lunch at the Café Pacific with a young girlfriend called Deborah, who was on the course with me. My afternoons were spent doing marketing research in the shopping precincts, shops and boutiques and finding out all the potential costs of going into business for myself. I also took a psychology course during this time, which I have found ever since to have been a great help when it comes to understanding the human condition and getting a different perspective on the people I meet.

During the morning I was a student, in the afternoon a potential business woman and in the evening a socialite, with all the local newspapers writing about me whenever I turned up anywhere, intrigued by the 'mysterious young woman from Europe'.

The woman from Merrill Lynch stayed in touch, sending me the prospectuses of properties now and then and I invited her and her husband to dinner. I also sent her a magnificent hand-made hat by Philip Sommerville to thank her for all her kindness and professional courtesy. No one was surprised that I had decided not to buy property because while I was there, in the autumn of 1987, the world's stock markets took a huge tumble, bringing property prices down with them. Texas was particularly badly hit, owing to the associated slump in oil prices. It was very lucky I hadn't invested as soon as I had arrived or I would have seen the value of my property drop by at least fifty percent.

One day I was about to have lunch with a girlfriend in the Mansion when I experienced one of those powerful feelings that hit you out of the blue. What on earth am I doing here in this place? I asked myself. I couldn't answer my own question, and the next day I began to arrange to return to London. In an instant I had completely changed my mind about my plans for Dallas. I stayed just long enough to honour my rental agreement on the apartment and finish the term at Miss Wade's, and within three weeks was back in St John's Wood. My sojourn in the USA had lasted less than a year.

Although I had been desperately keen to escape from the pressures and greyness of London into the uncomplicated, wide-open spaces of America, I had become homesick and was looking for an excuse to get back to my friends, whom I missed, along with all the culture and history embodied by Europe.

Once back in London I enrolled on a Fine Arts course at Sotheby's. It was lovely to be surrounded by a familiar culture once again and I resumed my travels around Europe, indulging a desire to see and enjoy everything on offer. About a year after Michael had died and before I went to Dallas I had made a trip to Spain. The Spanish were about to join the European Community and I envisaged huge possibilities for business projects. I thought that Madrid might be another possible venue for a fashion outlet that I had been considering even then, so I flew there to attend a fashion show organized by a friend of mine, a well-known designer from Valencia, Francis Montesinos, while exploring the possibilities of buying a property in the capital.

Frank Sinatra was giving a concert in Madrid at the time and I met one of his entourage at the Ritz, where I was staying, who very kindly sent me a couple of tickets and a bouquet of flowers. I was waiting for my driver outside the hotel one day and saw an extremely tall, slim man who was being addressed as 'Your Excellency' by the doorman. I didn't know who he was but a couple of days later, when flying back to London, we coincided at the airport and I noticed that he was looking at me. We fell into conversation and I discovered that his name was Thomas Enders and that he had formerly been the American Ambassador to Spain. When we boarded the aeroplane, I found that I was sitting next to an enormously fat man who looked as though he needed not only his own seat but mine as well. I called the stewardess.

'There is a gentleman a few seats in front of me with whom I should like to sit,' I told her. 'Would you be very sweet and see if you can arrange it please?' She very kindly complied and during the flight Thomas and I were able to get to know one another a little better. He told me that he had also been Chief of Mission in Cambodia and had played a key role in the Reagan administration's response to the Argentinian invasion of the Falkland Islands. Later I was to learn that he was also a trusted associate of Henry Kissinger and had served as Ambassador to Canada as well as what was then the EEC, before being appointed Assistant Secretary of State for Inter-American Affairs. When we reached London he took me home from the airport. He gave me his card, which showed his New York address, and I sent him a little thank-you note. This seemed to initiate a correspondence and although we were not to commence an intimate relationship until a few years later, whenever he came to London he took me out for dinner. I then didn't see him for nearly four years, although I often sent him little notes alerting him to my whereabout and telling him my news. I sometimes read about him in magazine and newspaper articles, some of which were not entirely flattering, and the more I read the more fascinated I became.

Four years down the line, I was in New York visiting a fashion house and Thomas paid a visit to my suite at the Plaza Athénée. By then he was senior director of Salomon Brothers, which at that time was probably the world's most powerful and profitable merchant bank. We took afternoon tea together and he then invited me to dinner the following day. From then on he called me every single day, whenever I was. He even phoned me at the airport as I was about to board Concorde to wish me *'bon voyage'*.

Thomas appeared to have become rather besotted with me. He was married to an Italian woman half his size and I was led to believe that their relationship was floundering somewhat – not that it particularly interested me. He continued to contact me daily in London, asking where and when we could meet again. We decided to rendezvous at the Château d'Esclimont, outside Paris, and I made all the arrangements. Two days before he was due to arrive he rang to say that he couldn't make it.

'You realize,' I told him, 'you will have to pay the Château a cancellation fee.' He started to make a big fuss about this comparatively small amount of money, which I thought was unbecoming and rather pathetic. This was a man who was phoning me very day, declaring his love, making huge government deals and working in one of the most senior positions in a company where billions of dollars were being traded in bonds every moment of the day, and yet he was making an issue out of such a minuscule payment. It seemed like the action of a cheap man to me and I lost much of my respect for him.

He continued his pursuit of me, however, and we met in Zurich a little later for what was supposed to be a three-day holiday together. He then told me that he had a meeting with the Kuwaiti Oil Minister. So we spent one day in Zurich, went to Vaduz in Liechtenstein for lunch and then I flew back to London on my own. I had made a big effort to be in Switzerland with him and I didn't think he was making much of an effort to be with me, which I found both insulting and annoying. I was not used to men who were not able and willing to take a few days off work when they wanted.

Despite his rather ungallant behaviour, Thomas seemed to be becoming keener and keener on our relationship and while we were in Zurich he had started to talk about the possibility of our having a child. He was a man in his mid-fifties and his three children were all grown-up. I could hear warning bells in the back of my mind. He seemed to me to be behaving like an overexcited child, but I decided to bide my time and see where the relationship led.

7

Becoming Lady Buck

In 1989, two years after returning from Texas, I was co-hosting a party with a friend, a bachelor called Jamal Izzet, in his house in Pavilion Road, Knightsbridge. Jamal, an Iraqi, was a lonely man in his late fifties who didn't have many close friends but who would spend a fortune entertaining shallow acquaintances who were happy to be on the receiving end of his hospitality. I had first met him at Les Ambassadeurs when we were both attending an event sponsored by Bulgari, the jewellers, where I had gone with a girlfriend. He told me his money came from deals he had done in Iraq, but I thought that was a little unlikely as he didn't strike me as being in possession of either a good business brain or much intelligence.

I suspected that Jamal was probably being looked after by family money. I also knew that at one stage he had been employed by the Saudi royal family to look after Prince Khaled when he was in London and wanted to go round the casinos, because I'd seen him once at the Ritz Casino years earlier when I was there having dinner with George Karam. He would have received a number of gifts and big tips for such work, as Saudis are renowned for their extreme generosity to those they like and to whom they feel obligated. But Jamal had an ability to upset people, for he had a short temper and was rather petulant and as a result had been banned from a number of restaurants and clubs as well as from Asprey.

Jamal's dinner parties were legendary. They were extremely lavish, with the highest-quality foods and wines, and the guests were always at their most elegant. Sadly, a number of these occasions were ruined for me by his behaviour, which could sometimes be rather boorish. He liked to give other people the impression that we were much closer than we actually were, doing things like getting up from the table to kiss me in front of his other guests. I remained polite but made it clear that this sort of thing was unacceptable to me. I certainly enjoyed being his co-hostess but wanted to be seen as an independent and unattached woman and not intimately associated with Jamal, which I wasn't.

One night there were twelve or fourteen guests. I remember Lady Rothermere, 'Bubbles', was there being very amusing and also Sir Antony Buck MP, who had accompanied Lady Olga Maitland. Lady Olga was then very involved in her Families for Defence campaign, of which Sir Antony was the patron. The dinner was being organized for her and because he was the eldest man there, etiquette demanded that Sir Antony sit on the right of the hostess, which was me. As far as I can remember, the rest of the guests that evening were the usual attendees but that didn't really matter to Jamal as long as he could fill all the seats around his table. I liked Bubbles. She was one of the few women in England who was genuinely glamorous and always great fun at parties.

Over dinner Sir Antony and I became friends. He was an infectiously kind and positive man. He had the most extraordinarily retentive memory and was able to recite poems and great tracts from history books with ease. However, he always seemed very keen to share his food with other people, which I thought rather vulgar, but he was obviously terribly excited about whatever it was he was eating and eager to have others try it. He reminded me a little of my father, who had died five years before, alone in his small house. Apparently it was several days before one of the neighbours discovered the body and I felt desperately sad that his life had ended in such a miserable way without my having made the effort to get to really know him. When Sir Antony talked about the way his ex-wife and grown family treated him, I felt that perhaps there were some similarities between them. My father ended his life as a sad and lonely man and I didn't want the same to happen to Sir Antony. I also wanted to get to know him because he was coming towards the end of a very interesting and successful career as a politician and had earlier been a very prominent criminal lawyer.

The next day I rang him at his office because I thought it might be nice to support Lady Olga's cause. I was finding that I had quite a bit of spare time on my hands and I had told Lady Olga that I would be delighted to help selling tickets for a concert that was being arranged to raise money. Sir Antony and I agreed to meet at the concert and it was after that event that we began to get together regularly for lunches and dinners, usually at the Houses of Parliament, but on occasion I would invite him to my flat. He seemed to be very popular with other MPs and anyone who knew him socially. Everybody thought he was great fun but didn't seem to take him terribly seriously because he drank so much. It must have been a difficult time for him, having gone through a divorce after being married for thirty-four years and now getting ready to retire from politics, which had been his whole life.

I could see that Sir Antony was a lonely man, despite his many friends. I also saw that he was very kind and generous to others, even though he was not wealthy, but that only very rarely did anyone seem to reciprocate. Many people took from him but few gave anything back. I think in return he found me a wonderful distraction, an interesting and amusing companion, and as I was totally independent I could be very generous towards him, as well as considerate and kind. We had fun together.

I was shocked to find what a very humble life he led. He lived in a tiny, simple, even dingy flat in Lambeth, with no luxuries or comforts at all. And as he had nothing but old and rather shabby clothes, I took him out and bought him some suits; this we both enjoyed, he as the recipient and I in making the gesture. Sadly I was to find out much later that sympathy is not a sufficient basis for a good, long-term relationship. Nonetheless, I had been planning to go to Monaco for a brief holiday, to stay in a suite at the Hôtel de Paris, right next to the Casino. I was also going to take the opportunity to look for an apartment for myself.

Thomas Enders was still around at this time even though I had been far from impressed with the way he had behaved towards me. He had made many promises of holidays and all the wonderful things he wanted to buy for me, none of which he ever kept. He had often been to my flat in London without ever bringing anything, not even a bunch of flowers. He definitely seemed to be rather mean and I was still waiting for him to prove himself worthwhile to me in some way. There had been several incidents which had made me doubt that he was the sort of man with whom I wanted to spend much time. For instance, we were dining at the Connaught one evening, when he spotted some Americans that he knew.

He was so frightened that they would see us together that he asked me to leave ahead of him, which seemed terribly cowardly and very ungallant. The next time he came to London and asked me where I wanted to go for dinner, which he always did, I told him that I wanted to return to the Connaught as it was so popular with Americans and I wanted him to feel at home. We went and this time I made sure that we left together.

Much the same thing happened in Zurich, at the Kronenhalle restaurant. I was very shocked and disappointed in him. No one had ever done that to me before. Usually men are very proud to have their friends see them with a person such as myself and just because a man is with an attractive woman who isn't his wife, does not necessarily mean that they are intimately involved. Another time he left his pyjamas in my apartment and then asked me to send them to him because his maid had missed them. Since when does a man have to answer to his maid?

I had been beginning to tire of London once again, even though my life was a great deal less hectic than it used to be, and I was seriously considering the possibility of starting a new life somewhere warm and beautiful, perhaps overlooking the sea. I had often invited girlfriends to accompany me on holiday as companions but on this occasion I thought it would be nice to invite Sir Antony to come to Monaco with me if he wasn't doing anything else, so that we might have a chance to develop our relationship. He was thrilled to accept because a group of his friends were going to be giving a party in Monaco which he had wanted to attend. I was quite happy to pay for everything because I didn't think it would be fair to impose heavy expenses on a man who was living in such a humble way. I knew that MPs made very little money and thought it would be courteous to pay for him.

I have always loved Monaco, with its luxury, beauty and high standards of excellence. Everything there is done in a grand and elegant style, as it is in much of the neighbouring South of France. I had been going to Monaco for some time because I had a lovely and charming mentor and friend there called Freddy, a very wealthy man and patron of the arts who was regarded as an institution in the principality and had made his fortune by being a major shareholder in Rio Tinto Zinc. He had a magnificent penthouse, where I used to stay with him, and we often dined at the Hôtel de Paris. Freddy was a widower in his sixties: his late wife, of whom he had been very fond, had died of cancer. Apparently I resembled her a great deal. He was a gentleman of the *ancien régime*, living like someone from the era of

Diaghilev and the Ballet Russe. He'd had a wide circle of friends, including Sartre, Misia, Onassis and Picasso. I wasn't quite as nice to Freddy as I ought to have been and once turned down an invitation from him to go to Geneva. When I heard of his death I regretted that, once again, I had been unable to thank a man for all his kindness.

Sir Antony and I had a lovely time but, being an insecure man and a bit of a child at heart, when we got back to England he told everybody in a rather indiscreet way all about the trip. For some reason Jamal was furious when he found out: probably because it shattered the impression he was trying to give everyone that the two of us were intimately involved. He seemed very jealous of my having taken Sir Antony to Monaco and he never found it in himself to forgive me. I told Sir Antony about Jamel knowing of the trip and he admitted that perhaps he had been rather indiscreet in his recounting the details of our time together but assured me that he had meant no harm. I forgave him, but the incident started little warning bells ringing which I really ought to have heeded.

In October 1989, six months after we met, Sir Antony and I became engaged to be married. His daughter, Louisa, an eminent writer on the arts who was about the same age as me, warned me about how insecure he was but in my conceit and supreme self-confidence I thought I would be able to change all that. I was thirty-one and I felt that perhaps it was about time to settle down and use some of the expertise that I had acquired over the years to build something different for myself. Sir Antony was about to retire from politics, and the Eastern Bloc countries, where he had made some very useful contacts owing to his former position as Naval Minister, were opening the doors to the West. He had no ideas about how he wanted to spend his retirement beyond the vague ambition to 'write some books', which I decided would not really be the right course for him. He particularly wanted to write a biography of a famous boxer of yesteryear, 'Gentleman' Jim Jackson.

'But Tony,' I reasoned with him, 'there is no money in writing books like that.' However, elderly people get very fixed ideas and it is hard to get them to change their mind, especially when there is a lot of alcohol involved. I was sure that with my help Sir Antony could change his outlook and do something constructive and profitable with the rest of his life.

Shortly before we got engaged I went to see my mother to tell her of my decision to marry Sir Antony. She counselled me against it, saying that the age gap between us of thirty years was bound to cause problems, but after a lot of persuasion on my part she agreed to meet him. We had dinner in the house in Chiswick where she was living with Paul, and invited her to the wedding. But she told us during the meal that she would feel uncomfortable and out of her depth at such an event and would prefer not to attend. The evening was not at all easy and in fact that dinner in late 1989 was the last time I ever saw my mother, for I had finally decided, after years of putting up with her unpleasantness and manipulation, that I had had enough.

I knew that Sir Antony was drinking heavily but I thought this was just because he was unhappy about his divorce and the pressures of his work as an active MP. I honestly thought that if I could change his life and make him happy and successful, then he would moderate his drinking. It is hard to change the habits of others, and only their wanting to do so can ever change anything, but I felt I had a very good chance of succeeding with Sir Antony because I thought that if I could offer him companionship, security, comfort and affection, then he would see the error of his ways.

I went to the House of Commons and on one occasion a colleague of Sir Antony's, John Butterfield, the MP for Plymouth and a charming and charismatic man, displayed a great deal of concern for my future husband. He confided in me that he and other members of the house had become seriously worried about Sir Antony's drinking, as well as his general health, and he told me that he seemed to be stumbling more and more when he walked. Noel Cochrane had become a friend of Sir Antony's through my introduction and when I told Noel of my intention to marry he said that he thought we might be good for one another and that if I were to make him happy, Sir Antony might well give up drinking. So I decided to go ahead with it and take an enormous step into the unknown.

The announcement of a forthcoming marriage between a distinguished MP of sixty-two and a beautiful and glamorous Spanish woman half his age created a storm of publicity in the media, fuelled by the fact that I was somebody new, somebody nobody knew about and somebody who had, until then, managed to keep her name out of the papers. I was overwhelmed by this sudden interest in my past and everything about me. I had always been a very private person and at first didn't see why I should have to speak about my life to anybody. Later I was accused of concealing my true origins from the world but I just couldn't see why I should tell journalists whom I'd never met before the most intimate details of my past. I wasn't interested in their lives, so why should they be interested in mine? I found it all extremely annoying but realized that it was going to be part of my role as an MP's wife. It was obviously something with which I would have to come to terms, and if I were to fulfil my role as expected, then I was determined to make a good job of it. Whenever journalists rang up asking for interviews, I dealt with them in a very professional manner, asking them what it was that they wished to interview me about and preparing imaginative questions for them in advance so that I was ready with the answers. In the end they were all very polite to me as I was no more than an attractive young woman marrying an elderly and distinguished MP and I felt very proud of the way I handled myself.

I wrote to Thomas Enders, telling him about my engagement to Sir Antony, and he reacted very badly. When we had been in Zurich towards the beginning of our relationship, he had offered to pay my travelling expenses. I had courteously refused the offer, wanting to show him that I was both financially independent and perfectly capable of looking after myself. I also told him that if he wanted to give me anything it would have to be something a great deal more impressive than that. He insisted, however, and wrote to me later enclosing his American Express credit card number. Subsequently I made a further two trips to New York on Concorde and a visit to Zurich, and on each occasion he suddenly found that he was unable to meet me. When he heard that I was going to marry Sir Antony, he wrote to me saying that he had no intention of paying for these trips which I had charged to his card, as after all he was the one not to show up and not me.

'Fine,' I told him, 'we'll sort it out in court.' So, armed with the letter he had signed giving me the number of his card as well as his instructions to use it, I went to my solicitor, knowing full well that I couldn't possibly lose. I also knew that Thomas would not want the publicity which a court case would inevitably generate. He must have been advised that he had no case and I never heard anything more about it. Although I had won this little skirmish I still felt very angry at the way he had behaved. He had written me many love letters, telling me how much he adored me and how he wanted us to have a child. In these same letters he gossiped about secret government deals with which he was involved and revealed some of the intimate adventures he had witnessed on the private jet of a Kuwaiti government minister. He had breached every confidence imaginable in these breathless missives, relinquishing any last claim he might have had to my respect and loyalty.

•   •   •

In the New Year I invited Sir Antony to spend a few days with me at the beautiful Imperial Hotel in Vienna. I also invited a friend of mine called Mira Milan, who was the manageress of Ungaro in London and someone for whom I'd done some fashion promotions. I knew that she was looking for a husband, so I asked my old friend Joseph Tadros, with whom I was still in touch, to join us after Sir Antony had gone back to England. I knew that Joseph had a very handsome and eligible unmarried brother in Athens whom I thought Mira ought to meet. From London I had managed to book seats at the Vienna Opera and I very much enjoyed seeing *Aida* with Sir Antony and later *Tosca* with Joseph. Sir Antony had a rather tasteless habit of always commenting on other women's looks, saying things like 'She's a bit of all right', which I considered to be in extremely bad taste given that we were now engaged. I told him that I didn't like him talking that way but he just laughed as if I was the one being foolish. We spent a lot of time walking around the quiet streets of Vienna at night, talking all the time. He seemed to be very interested in my finances, which concerned me a little. He wanted to know exactly how much money I had in the bank but I revealed nothing to him. I certainly didn't want him to marry me for my money.

Sir Antony and I saw the New Year in at a wonderful ball in the hotel. On New Year's day I arranged for us to have a romantic lunch outside Vienna in a restaurant up in the woods. Before the lunch we went to listen to the Vienna Boy's Choir and attend Mass in the same church. At the end of the service all the boys came down to take communion. It was a beautiful and magical sight.

After Sir Antony had left and before Joseph's arrival, Mira and I were talking in the hotel and she asked if Joseph knew that I was engaged to Sir Antony. I hadn't told him and we then came up with an idea to see if he still felt the same way about me as he used to. We selected an incredible and outrageously expensive diamond ring from a top jeweller in Vienna and when Joseph arrived I asked him to buy it for me. It still felt that there might be time to break off my engagement to Sir Antony and marry Joseph if he made it worth my while. He didn't actually say no. What he said was that before buying me the ring he would have to talk to his family about our getting married. I regarded this as a rather feeble excuse not to get engaged there and then and to acquire the ring on the spot. I became unnecessarily aggressive towards Joseph, who was totally taken aback by my behaviour even though it was obvious that he was till extremely fond of me. I had the feeling that I had heard all the same delaying tactics from Michael before he died and wasn't intending to go through all that again. Sadly, I said some rather unpleasant things and the two of us parted on bad terms.

If Joseph had said yes I would most certainly have married him and not Sir Antony, and the next few years of my life would have been very different indeed, although living in Khartoum would not have been my ideal wish given the problems that existed there at the time.

My wedding to Sir Antony took place in March 1990 and Noel Cochrane gave me away. After the civil ceremony at Westminster Register Office, we took a few friends to lunch at the Oxford and Cambridge Club. From there Sir Antony and I drove to Cliveden, in Buckinghamshire, a quiet, elegant and beautiful country hotel converted from the former home of the Astors. The following day we would be flying out to Barbados. I was taking care of all the expenses and arrangements and had no idea of the nightmare which was about to engulf my life.

8

Trapped in a Nightmare

Almost as soon as we started our honeymoon I realized what a horrible mistake I had made. I had chosen Barbados because Concorde flew there at the time of the year and as Sir Antony had never flown on Concorde before I thought it would be a nice treat as well as a fun trip for him. I booked us in for a week at the Royal Pavilion, which, I was told, was one of the best and most luxurious hotels in the Caribbean. Hakim was being very sweet and was still caring for me even though I had not told him about my plans to marry Sir Antony, which was rather cruel. He had been obliged, like everyone else, to find out about the wedding from the newspapers and television news. I hadn't told him because I had known perfectly well that he would not approve, but I didn't know how to break it to him without hurting his feelings. He had been very understanding and forgiving and never reprimanded me for this discourtesy, remaining his usual kind and supportive self. It was a sign of his unfaltering and eternal friendship for me.

Even on the flight, Sir Antony was beginning to drink and make lewd remarks about some of the other female passengers, commenting on them to me with really choice phrases like 'She's a bit of good news', which I found very insulting towards me. If anyone was 'good news', it was me, his bride, a beautiful and elegant woman thirty years his junior. I became extremely angry with him and told him that he was behaving very badly.

'Oh, don't start making a fuss now,' he said. 'And for heaven's sake stop nagging me!'

I had a sick feeling in the pit of my stomach. I definitely did not like the idea of being associated with someone who was behaving so badly and I suddenly had this very clear vision that rather than my being able to help him with his drinking problem as had been my firm intention, it was going to get a good deal worse. I began to imagine how it would be if he continued to behave like he was doing on the plane, in front of my friends and contacts, and in professional and social situations. I had often heard him being indiscreet about other people at dinner parties and, although I did not think it was in good taste to talk in that way, I had been willing to put up with it as long as it was not our private life that he was gossiping and joking about so flagrantly. I had been seriously concerned when I found he had been recounting our Monaco trip as if it were no more than an amusing anecdote, but had hoped that, when he saw how hurt I was by that incident, he would be more careful in the future. What he'd been doing in fact was boasting to anyone and everyone how he had been taken to Monte Carlo by me, how I had picked up the tab for everything and how well it reflected on him that he was still able to get women to pay for his company at this late stage in his life.

By now I was beginning to fear that if his drinking continued then so would his tendency to blab his mouth off, and that was something I hated. The whole philosophy of my life's success had been built up on the basis of discretion and now it appeared that the very opposite quality was about to destroy it. I had suddenly become very vulnerable and I was aware that in the future, if we were to proceed with our plans to develop Sir Antony's professional and business contacts after he retired from parliament, he would be in a position to cause me a great deal of harm. I didn't like this situation but hadn't been able to foresee it before my decision to marry.

With the benefit of hindsight, it is very clear to me that what I saw above all else in Sir Antony was simply a substitute father figure. Rosa had been the first person to really bring this to my attention and I had somehow allowed her to convince me that here was this elderly man whom I was going to help with his life and to whom I could offer companionship, comfort and affection – all the things I had been unable to offer my own father. In other words, here was someone I could help, whereas I had been unable to help my poor father. Suddenly it was all becoming terribly clear to me while I was on my honeymoon.

I have always considered it a sign of great insecurity when mature people joke too much and make silly remarks all the time in order to make themselves popular. These are invariably the same people who betray confidences to others in order to endear themselves and I believe that such people always end up making fools of themselves as well as being a menace to others. If they are public figures they ought to be even more careful about what they say, for fear that one day it may be either misconstrued or used against them. If I was going to be in business with Sir Antony by my side I needed to be sure that I could rely on him to behave correctly among professional people. When he was sober he was always delightful company but it was suddenly very clear to me that in the future these times were going to be in the minority.

So here I was at the beginning of my honeymoon already regretting that I had married only two days previously. I had never been to the Caribbean before and the island of Barbados was a big disappointment to me, seeming primitive and dirty. The food at the hotel was drab and unimaginative, the weather dreadful because it was off-season and after two days I'd had enough. Sir Antony was behaving most oddly and I can only suppose that having me on his arm aroused some long-dormant desire to both flaunt and try to assert his masculinity. Thus, although he was sixty-two at the time, he tried to water-ski, which was both an embarrassment and a disaster. He was also continuing to behave in a totally boorish way and I tried to cut the trip short only to discover that there were no readily available flights and that therefore we were obliged to stay the whole week.

There were, of course, the less trying and even enjoyable moments, such as the trip on the small submarine to see the marine flora and fauna and the yacht which we hired to take us around the islands. But I was not really in a position to fully appreciate all these things. I had realized that not only had I signed away all the freedom and independence for which I had fought so hard, but also when we returned to England, the man to whom I suddenly seemed to find myself married would be coming into my home, into my private space. Never, in all of my adult life had I been obliged to share my living quarters with anyone else apart from my mother. Sir Antony was not really even considering paying for the honeymoon and I didn't want him to think that he could continue to rely on my financial generosity for ever. It was to be a further three months before I managed to tackle the subject with the delicacy and tact which I felt were appropriate.

By the time we arrived back in London I was totally convinced of my error in marrying Sir Antony and was seriously distressed about the uncertainty of my future. I woke up at five o'clock in the morning of our first day back and stared miserably out of the balcony door while Sir Antony slept on in my bed. I started to cry, feeling very sorry for myself, knowing that I was trapped and had allowed a degree of compassion, which until then I had deliberately subdued all my life, to overcome my true sense of purpose and my desire for independence. I had nowhere to run and hide. My advice to any woman entering a long-term relationship or marriage is always to insist on having enough space so as to allow yourself room to breathe and be alone when it becomes necessary. Ideally there should be enough room in the marital home for you to have your own set of rooms. I had had such a beautiful lifestyle and now all I could see was a ball and chain around my ankle. I wouldn't be able to move or breathe without Sir Antony knowing about it. Not that I had any intention or plans to do anything secretive, but a woman should always be able to keep some parts of her life private and exclusive. Looking back on all the kind, dignified, affluent and powerful men I had known in the past, I suddenly realized just how much I had given up. I had shed my old life as if it were no more than a cocoon, almost on a whim, and now I was going to miss it painfully.

I waited until Sir Antony had left for Westminster that morning and then rang Hakim and asked him to come over. 'Be patient,' he counselled me when I had poured out my heart to him. 'Give yourself at least a year before you decide what to do and if things don't work out you can then ask for a divorce.' He was very concerned about me but also about my financial situation, which would be severely compromised were a divorce to take place. However, my finances were the last thing on my mind at that stage and I would have paid anything to get out of my predicament.

There was also the likelihood that, should a separation or even divorce ensue from our marriage too soon, it would be extremely detrimental to Sir Antony, towards whom I bore no malice, as well as to me. So, taking Hakim's advice, I pulled myself together, put on a smile and got on with the job in hand. As the wedding has been attended by only a very few close friends, Sir Antony and I decided to host a dinner celebration for about thirty people in a private room at the Connaught. I chose a fabulous menu with the choicest wines and took care of all the invitations and arrangements. Sir Geoffrey Howe, a lovely man and an old friend of Sir Antony's, sat on my right and Hakim on my left. What amazed me was that most of the guests, though fully aware of the reason for the celebration, arrived at the wedding dinner empty-handed. The wife of one MP, Sir Robert Rhodes-James, gave me a tiny ashtray, which I thought was incredibly mean and a dreadful insult. I had never encountered behaviour from such people before, and even the working-class folk I had lived among as a child in Spain were generous at times such as weddings and birthdays. I was appalled at their lack of dignity and *savoir-faire*. I don't think Sir Antony really noticed; he just continued being affable and joking with everyone.

There were a number of incidents over the years which highlighted the myth of the hospitality and generosity of the upper classes. Indeed I never ceased to be surprised at the lack of these qualities, but it proved an interesting education. On one occasion Sir Antony and I were invited to a charity dinner party and concert given by the MP Toby Jessel's wife, who had met me only once. The invitation came completely out of the blue. I was telephoned and told that they were organizing some sort of event and thinking of their 'best friends' and were asking us to pay £75 each for the privilege of their company. Again, I gave a lot of my time and money to Lady Olga Maitland's personal cause, Families for Defence, and even went to her home, yet after she invited me to a reception I arrived to find that I was expected to pay to get in. Although the other invitees were also asked to pay, I left as I did not think that this was the right way to behave towards guests.

I was very eager for Sir Antony to retire from politics so that together we could start to organize his future as a potential adviser to the former Eastern Bloc. It was my opinion that, with new countries emerging from under the cloak of the dismantled Soviet Union, there would be a strong demand for experienced statesmen and politicians to help smooth the way to democracy, as well as all kinds of opportunities for trade agreements and lucrative commercial contracts. I called Sir Antony's secretary, Jane, to whom I was later very generous, and asked her to keep a careful record of everyone that my husband met in the course of his work and our very hectic political social life, because he might well be needing access to these people later on. If there was one thing I understood by now, it was the importance of building a network of contacts. If the plan worked, Sir Antony would not be retiring into years of boredom and frustration, but would be able to progress smoothly from national politics to much greater things in the international arena.

Until his retirement happened, however, it was business as usual as a

British politician, and I was determined to do a good job of supporting him in his work. It was just after we got engaged that I had first visited Sir Antony's constituency in Colchester, Essex, and it was there that I discovered just how high he stood in the esteem of all his constituents. They knew him to be a good, kind person, concerned with their welfare and, as a man of integrity and sincerity, more than capable of representing their interests in Westminster. It was for these reasons that he was so highly respected. I felt very proud to have married such a good man and at moments like that I felt a great hope that we could build an exciting future together.

My first formal engagement with Sir Antony was a dinner at Colchester Town Hall, where he introduced me as his fiancée to all the local community dignitaries. It was from that moment that everyone, especially the media, became interested in me and my life, although before this I had never even been in the newspapers other than when I was in Dallas. There is no doubt that I was rather different from the types of wives normally associated with politicians. I had chosen to look very glamorous for the event and there was certainly no one in the room dressed like me. I suspect that many of the guests felt that I ought to adapt my style and tone myself down so as to fit into my new role. But from the beginning I had no intention of falling into line with other people's ideas of how I should be. They were all very surprised and curious, wanting to see and meet the new woman in Sir Antony's life. I found them all to be wonderful, although I doubt that I was quite what any of them was expecting.

From the outset, I always dressed elegantly and far better than the wives and women who gathered in and around Westminster. I remember that, on one occasion when I was wearing a beautiful hat and gloves to accompany my outfit and awaiting my husband in the Central Hall at Westminster, one MP's wife came up to me and said, 'Oh, are we at Ascot?'

'No, my dear,' I purred, 'we are at lunch.'

Such small-minded and judgemental people could not possibly change or even influence me but they made it hard for me to grow in the environment of being a politician's wife. Did they not know that for centuries no lady of position or breeding would have considered for a moment lunching out without a hat and had not Lady Astor, the first female MP, been a prime exponent of that fashion? Just because their only experience of dressing-up was for the odd wedding or Ascot week, that didn't mean that I should compromise my sartorial standards.

I wanted to help my husband in every aspect of his work. I felt he deserved to be successful and I also enjoyed the job of being his wife. Busy MPs cannot be in two places at once, and so Sir Antony couldn't be representing his constituents in Westminster and meeting people in Colchester at the same time. Therefore I took a number of trips to the constituency on my own to represent him at local events such as fêtes or the opening of new offices. Several of these I attended with a local businessman, Ronnie Lancaster of Lancaster Motors, one of the largest dealerships of luxury cars in the country and now part of the Jardine Group of Companies. Ronnie was a stylish and charming man, very kind and correct, although I suspect he was a little in love with me and on one occasion sent me a superb orchid tied with a gold ribbon. I thought it very charming but in no way did I encourage him to think that we ever enjoyed anything other than a platonic friendship.

One particularly enjoyable event was when, purely by coincidence, Halcrow's, the firm of consulting engineers for whom I used to work, decided to open an office in Colchester. It was at the opening of that branch, at which I represented my husband, that I had the pleasure of meeting and talking with the Duke of Gloucester.

Within a short time of our getting married, Sir Antony's possessiveness and jealousy began to show through. I never once gave him any reason to believe that I was anything but faithful to him other than the affair with Sir Peter Harding, which was much later on. The feelings that Sir Antony began to display were entirely due to his own insecurity and certainly never stemmed from anything that I said or did. But the truth was that, whenever I took a trip on my own or did anything, Sir Antony would accuse me viciously of having affairs with other men the moment I was out of his sight, and often used phrases like 'rent-a-wife' when referring to me on social occasions. His behaviour made my life and work impossible because I could not rely on him to behave correctly in company and I always knew that if I took any initiative on my own I would be accused of doing things behind his back.

On top of this, because he was an MP and had been a Navy Minister, I was constantly frightened that the IRA would target him with a bomb. I often told him of my worries but he shrugged them off, refusing to take any security precautions. I would get up at one or two in the morning, when he usually returned from Parliament, and would go downstairs to check for snipers outside and for car bombs. I even used to get down on my hands and knees in order to examine the chassis of the Jaguar before we could go out in it. And then there were all the efforts of the security services, who were incredibly helpful and supportive in installing many specialized sensory devices as well as an alarm in my apartment. I thought that, as my husband, Sir Antony should be as concerned for my peace of mind as I was for his security and that he should at least make some effort to take care of his safety as a potential target.

A few months after we were married, I was invited to the opening of a new nightclub in Colchester called Valentino's. It was run by a couple called Michael and Angela, both of whom had formerly been police officers. Although Sir Antony didn't think that it was appropriate for an MP's wife to attend the opening, I thought that I was the perfect person to attend and that, by being enterprising, Michael and Angela were doing something beneficial for the young people in the community. I wanted to help them get going in any way that I could and thought that it would be a good idea at the same time to raise some money for a charity such as the Cheshire Homes, one of which was nearby. I knew of the existence of the Seven Rivers Home, because it was at one of its fêtes that I made my début representing Sir Antony. I started to think what I could do to make an impact and create some publicity for the nightclub while at the same time raising money for such a good cause. I decided to select some of the finest hats from the collection of the renowned milliner Philip Sommerville and then build a fashion show around them. I also involved a local boutique, which was happy to supply the clothes in return for the publicity.

I worked very hard for the event, choosing the music, all the clothes and hats, and giving away one of my hats as a prize. I had the invitations and programmes printed on pure cotton paper which I ordered from Dallas with a gold seal embossed at the top. I ended up topping and tailing over five hundred invitations, including a personal message in each. Eventually, Philip Sommerville not only lent us his collection but also gave us as another prize the prototype of the veil worn by the Princess of Wales for the enthronement of the Crown Prince Akihito of Japan. I ordered little perfume bottles from the famous Parisian perfumier Annik Goutal, and these were all wrapped in cellophane and tied with gold bows as gifts for both men and women. On the day, I greeted all the guests and presented the programme myself, of which I was justifiably very proud.

Standing on the stage in the spotlight, beautifully dressed, gave me a wonderful feeling and it briefly called to mind my long-buried childhood ambitions to be an actress like my then idol Marisol.

Sir Antony escorted me to the show, to which I had invited a number of important figures from the Spanish Embassy. Also among the guests was Ronnie Lancaster. I enjoyed the whole thing enormously and Sir Antony told me that he was very proud of me. Just for a moment, with the music and applause still ringing in my ears, I thought perhaps that Hakim had been right and I only needed to give the marriage time, a period to allow Sir Antony and myself to become accustomed to our mutually changed circumstances and find a way of living together in harmony. I felt very proud of myself and happy to be with my husband at such a successful occasion.

The feeling of elation was short-lived, however. There were, of course, other good days, but in general our relationship became increasingly sour over the ensuing year. During the parliamentary recesses Sir Antony always seemed to be in my flat, drinking heavily and smoking his infernal cigars. There were stains on the carpets, burns and damaged furniture in the home which I had worked so hard to create and the stink of tobacco everywhere. He was a very messy and disorganized man. I would carefully clear up his desk for him and he would then go and mess it up again. I was exhausted, doing everything I could to make him happy, trying to be flexible and accommodating but making myself very unhappy in the process.

Over the years I have come to like neatness, order and beauty in my life. I can't bear to have damaged things around me and would rather throw them away. All around me crystal glasses were getting broken and tables scratched. I couldn't bear it. I have always made a point of looking after my possessions and once, when I was passing through Customs and Immigration with a beautiful crocodile vanity case, one of the officers stopped me and asked where and when I had purchased it.

'This old thing? I've had it for months,' I offered.

'It looks just like new,' he said suspiciously.

'That's because I take special care when handling my beautiful belongings,' I said, smiling, then added provocatively, 'Just as I wear gloves whenever I put on my stockings,' and tottered off, leaving him speechless.

Although I look after my possessions, I also like to be able to get rid of them as soon as they become superfluous or I tire of them. I hate clutter and mementoes of all kinds and have always gone for the minimalist look, with a lot of glass, marble and black lacquer furniture. As a result my homes tend to look like show flats or Oriental museums rather than somewhere where anyone lives.

Because my marriage was making me unhappy and I was no longer able to do anything without incurring the temper of my husband, my health began to suffer. I too began to drink to escape from the reality of what had happened to my life; a little at first and then increasingly more, mostly champagne and wine, but later vodka as well. I drank mainly so that I could feel drowsy enough to sleep, but, because my mind was troubled and in turmoil, I found it hard to sleep and gradually the amount I required increased. Eventually I was sleeping for twelve hours at night as well as three to four hours in the afternoon, having started to drink early in the morning. That way the hours could slip by with my knowing that nothing exciting or interesting was ever going to happen. Not completely beyond the ability to reason, I decided that I needed to get out and find something to occupy my mind. This I did, but the seeds of alcoholism were sown and despite my efforts to decrease the volume, I found it increasingly difficult to either sleep or get through my waking hours without having to rely on alcohol.

I had read in French *Vogue* that a Parisian hairdresser called Naim was opening a salon in Knightsbridge, backed by a businessman from central Africa. I mentioned this to my own hairdresser, Anthony Cooper, whom I'd first met when I used to have my hair done at Claridge's but who was now freelance. I suggested that he might think about approaching them for a permanent position. He did that and when I went to see him at the salon I was introduced to the owners. They invited me out to dinner and were obviously interested in some of my comments regarding the salon itself. They admitted that they were having troubles with the business and asked if I would consider managing it for them and sorting out the problems. I thought that this would be an interesting challenge and at the same time get me out of the apartment, where Sir Antony had installed himself during the parliamentary summer recess.

When I started to look into their problems, however, I realized that things were quite bad. Having been given the licence to do as I saw fit, I set about preparing a business plan and marketing scheme for the relaunch of the business. The day came when I put my proposals, all sound and carefully laid out, to the owners. But regrettably they were not prepared to entertain my plans or sink any further capital into the business. I told them nicely that if they were not going to accept my proposals then I would have no alternative but to terminate my contract with them, which I did after having been there for only a month. They promptly closed down the salon. It had been an interesting, if not successful, experience and an opportunity to put to good use some of the business experience I had gained over the years. But it had been very stressful and trying during that month, having Sir Antony at home and dashing back to make him lunch and check that he was all right and hadn't set the flat on fire with one of his cigars.

The one advantage of my new domesticated set-up was that I was at last able to indulge myself and get a puppy. In fact I bought two King Charles spaniels, a Tri-colour and a Blenheim, and called them Coco and Pebbles. I absolutely adored them from the moment they arrived and over the next couple of years they were the only loves in my life.

On the political and social side, things were no more exciting. The other wives of MPs and Ministers with whom I was having a deal horrified me. They were all terribly insular, drab and totally out of touch with the international political arena. A lot of them were quite patronizing to me, telling me 'how exciting' it must be for me to go to garden parties at Buckingham Palace or to receptions at Numbers Ten and Eleven Downing Street.

I recall a royal garden party where I was milling around with the other guests while Sir Antony smiled and waved to the people he knew. An usher approached and asked me if I would like to be introduced to the Queen. 'No, thank you,' I replied, explaining that I felt a little unwell. In fact I was fine. I just had no interest in meeting Her Majesty at such a crowded event and felt that, if I were to have the pleasure, I should prefer it to be on an occasion with far fewer people. As for some of the other people I came across, I must say that I have never regarded a mere handshake and patronizing small talk from anyone high-born as a suitable reward for anything I might ever do, and unless they are people who have achieved something with their lives in their own right, titles cut no ice with me at all.

I was equally disenchanted with the people I met in Downing Street, but with some exceptions. Margaret Thatcher, I thought, was one of the greatest leaders the British have ever had and grew more beautiful with the years. She was aloof and always kept her distance, with her light handshake and glazed eyes. There was nothing warm or personable about her, which is exactly the right attitude for the leader of a major world power after ten years in office. Denis, her husband, was delightful and I thought they made an excellent couple, balancing each other perfectly. John Major was gentle, a man of great courage and conviction, making everyone feel comfortable around him at Number Ten, which I always thought seemed like a cosy, typical English house.

I had always admired Michael Heseltine in the past as having some flair and charisma, but when I met him he seemed devoid of all charm, although not as bad as Douglas Hurd, who seemed terribly intimidated by me or any other woman for that matter, was insecure, always shabbily dressed and likewise lacked any charm. I liked Ken Livingstone very much, and Lord Home, whom I had first met when I was an impressionable young girl under the wing of Lady Edith Bird, was charismatic and very warm. Both men were charming and seemed to be human beings in their own right and not puppets dancing to the tunes of others.

A good many of the political figures whom I met during my marriage to Sir Antony were, sadly, rather let down by their wives. It seemed that they had all married exactly the same 'twin-set and pearls' type who wore sensible shoes and were guaranteed not to scare the horses. That's all very well if you're not moving in society's more elevated circles. But they were the wives of leading statesmen and politicians and had no style, worldiness or elegance in any way and were desperately dull to talk to. I respect the right of people to simplicity but charm and elegance are a by-product of confidence and this is still very much needed in politics today, if not from the politicians themselves then at least from their wives.

Because Sir Antony had been at Cambridge with Sir Geoffrey Howe, we saw more of him than most of the Cabinet. When he was Deputy Prime Minister, we were invited down to his official country residence one weekend just for the day, which meant staying for lunch and dinner. It was a very typical English country house and the other guests included Peter and Virginia Bottomley and Richard Giordano, the very powerful chairman of BOC and for a long time the best-paid executive in Britain. He was a very charming and elegant man who seemed rather cautious and, again, a little intimidated by me. We had a light lunch and then during the afternoon sat by the pool. I was very tired and wanted to sleep but because of the number of house guests there wasn't a spare bedroom. Sir Antony and I had been asked to use the Howes' bedroom but I didn't like the idea of sleeping on someone else's bed. The whole thing was very poorly arranged and there was a ghastly and badly behaved little Yorkshire terrier called Budget which kept snapping at everyone.

Dinner was a formal, sit-down affair, for which I wore a particularly glamorous dress. Having sat down to dinner, I was absolutely appalled when they served stew! I suspect that even Coco and Pebbles would have turned their noses up at that. After this questionable prandial treat, all the women went upstairs to powder their noses or wash their hands or something. Even Virginia Bottomley, one of the most senior politicians of the day, was willing to do this. I had never allowed myself to be fobbed off like some second-class citizen and certainly didn't intend to start now, so I simply joined the men in the drawing-room, figuring that I was their guest and therefore had just as much right to coffee and cognac as anyone else.

Richard Giordano seemed utterly taken aback, but at the same time rather impressed. 'You're the only woman I've met who has ever done this,' he protested.

'Well,' I replied, 'I have no intention of going off with the wives of these other people as if I was a frightened rabbit. And I don't want to be seen condoning a tradition that in my view demeans women.'

I recall that on the way back home that evening Sir Antony said to me, 'That was very daring, my love.' I didn't think so.

9

The Centre of Power

I met Air Chief Marshal Sir Peter Harding in September 1990, at a dinner party in London hosted by the then Indian High Commissioner. Sir Peter was seated on my right but for most of the dinner I was concentrating on helping the man on my left, a disabled gentleman and member of the House of Lords, who was there with his wife. I noticed that Sir Peter was a very impressive man, tall and attractive, but we spoke only briefly, although during that time he did flirt with me, albeit in a fairly innocent way. After dinner I joined the men as usual for coffee and liqueurs, refusing an invitation to join the ladies. I must have made an impression on Sir Peter because a couple of months later he invited my husband and I to a dinner at his official residence in Kingsley Court, Knightsbridge. Sir Antony and I had to leave the dinner early, however, because the next day, 6 November, was the day of the fashion show in Colchester. Sir Peter's flat, supplied for him by the government, was very comfortable but decorated in a typically English way, with lots of frills and heavy, wooden furniture.

It was February the following year when I next met Sir Peter and Lady Harding, again at a dinner party. By then the Allies were at war with Saddam Hussein and Sir Peter was the Chief of Defence. He and I sat next to each other, but, apart from touching my hand once, he behaved with perfect discretion. I was very careful to keep the conversation light and courteous as I didn't want him to feel in the least bit uneasy with his wife and Sir Antony there.

On this occasion Sir Peter asked me how he might get in touch with me and we exchanged private telephone numbers. I thought it would be a great idea to get to know him better. He was, after all, in an enormously powerful position at the time and could have proved useful as a contact for my husband and I with all his military experience, once Sir Antony had retired. I also thought, with all my contacts in the Middle East, that we could discuss business plans and possible introductions which might be of mutual interest to us. I didn't at that stage know exactly how we could work together, but I imagined there might be something interesting we could do, perhaps connected with arms sales or military engineering projects. The first step was to get to know him better, without Sir Antony around to cause a distraction with his silly and inane banter.

A few days later I called Sir Peter at his office and invited him to lunch at the Connaught Hotel. So as not to compromise him, I invited a lady friend to join us. I thought that Sir Peter might feel uneasy to be seen in a hotel, lunching alone with a young woman who was looking very glamorous in a hat and gloves. Many senior government figures eat at the Connaught and it was very likely that both of us would be recognized by the other guests.

We had a beautiful lunch, during which Sir Peter impressed me as a kind, sensitive and thoughtful man, someone with whom I should like to be better acquainted. Afterwards my 'chaperone' made her excuses and left. I discreetly settled the bill outside the restaurant, as I always do when I am with guests, and Sir Peter and I went through to the drawing-room for coffee.

We talked a little more and then I stood up. 'I am going to do this,' I told him, and kissed him on the lips. I was still wearing my beautiful hat and I thought it would seem like something unusual and different for him. He was distinguished-looking and gentle, and it was obvious that we were very attracted to each other. He told me that, were anything to develop, I must never reveal our relationship to anyone. I was a little offended that he even felt he had to mention it, but I assumed that he was just a little innocent of the ways of the world and assured him that the secret was quite safe. I had no more wish to incur Sir Antony's wrath than he had to upset Lady Harding and his family, or endanger his career. Neither of us had anything to gain by being indiscreet.

A few days later he called me and we met for dinner at the elegant

Belvedere restaurant in Holland Park. I had brought along my second Jaguar, this time the more powerful XJRS which Sir Antony enjoyed driving, but on this occasion I had borrowed a chauffeur for the evening. It was the first car I'd had since the Ferrari and I enjoyed owning it very much. The evening was not quite as relaxed as I had planned because Sir Peter was in a sombre mood. The understandable reason for his solemnity was that it was the day that the first dead British servicemen's bodies and other casualties had been brought back from the Gulf.

'This is the first time I have received my men back in coffins,' he told me. Nonetheless he was very attentive and charming, telling me what a wonderful, interesting and beautiful woman I was and how excited he was to be with me. Once more he told me not to mention our relationship to anyone, which again I thought was totally unnecessary. We talked briefly about Sir Antony. I said what a nice man my husband was and how I felt my role in his life was to support him as an MP's wife, but I told him nothing of the problems I was having with our marriage.

I was also careful not to ask too much about Sir Peter's work at such an early stage in the relationship. We were there to get to know each other and I didn't want him to feel that he was being subjected to a cross-examination. If the relationship looked like developing into an affair, that would be when I would start to do my homework on the subjects which were of interest to him. For the first few dates, it is always wise for a woman to spend a lot of time listening to what the man has to say, remaining calm, interested, charming and not remotely judgemental. Also, I always avoid questioning men about their private lives. In this case I knew that Sir Peter was married because I had met him and his wife socially, but normally I would make a habit of never enquiring on a first meeting about a man's marital status or whether or not he had children. I think that it is very vulgar to ask such questions and it is usually a waste of time anyway as men rarely, if ever, tell the truth. I wanted to find out what he was like and what his ambitions were. In fact he was very uncertain as to what the future might hold for him. He had been expecting to be retired at the end of his term as Air Chief Marshal, not realizing that the Gulf war would come along and that he would later be promoted to Chief of Defence.

After dinner we went for a little walk in the restaurant's romantic gardens and he kissed me intimately for the first time. He was very charming. I could see that he was falling in love with me and it felt good to know that I had lost none of my abilities or allure. Living with Sir

Antony, I had begun to wonder if my former life had all been a dream or a fantasy, such was the ease with which I fell into the role of a wife to a serving MP. I dropped Sir Peter in Knightsbridge and the chauffeur drove me home through Hyde Park.

After this first private meeting he began to write me beautiful love letters, full of compliments and telling me how much he thought of me, how special I was and how he would always remember our first kiss and was looking forward to us being together to share our emotions and feelings. They were lovely to receive, because Sir Antony was out a lot of the time and I was beginning to feel a little neglected. I wrote back politely acknowledging the letters but in nowhere near as fulsome or graphic a tone.

Sir Peter and I met about once a month to start with and more often than not I would be the one who paid for our lunch or dinner. I didn't want him to compromise himself by putting his name on hotel or restaurant reservations or bills. He said that he wished he could pay for more but that he did not have much money. Only later did I discover that he was earning a six-figure salary as well as receiving luxury accommodation and his family's living costs, all at the taxpayers' expense. I did not question the arrangement at the beginning because I was quite happy to pay. I was quite comfortable doing so as it had always been the case in the past when I was pursuing a particular ambition. My ultimate plan was for me to work with him once he had left the military in the capacity of a public relations adviser. It gave me pleasure to be in control and I felt that it would help the business side of our relationship if he understood that I was a woman of substance.

I did, however, begin to notice that his stinginess and lack of style ran rather deeper than mere expediency. He used to send me flowers through a telephone service but the blooms which arrived were dreadful. I said nothing to begin with but eventually I just had to speak. 'Peter,' I said, 'the flowers which are being delivered to me are appalling.' He was horrified and from then on went to Harrod's to pick out all the flowers personally. Just another example of how a woman is nearly always obliged to show men exactly how she wishes to be treated before they are able to understand it for themselves.

Our meetings were so infrequent that I thought it might be nice for the two of us to go away together to spend some time in one another's company. I suggested that we should go to the Villa d'Este on Lake Como, where I used to spend my summer holidays with my dear friend George Karam. I told Sir Peter how wonderfully romantic the place was and offered to buy the tickets. He was exchanted with the idea. After I had done this, however, I had second thoughts. I remembered the reaction I got after taking Sir Antony with me to Monte Carlo. I decided it would be imprudent and inappropriate because I was now a married woman, so I cancelled the trip. To console him for his disappointment, I bought Sir Peter a beautiful fountain pen from the Cartier Panther range. I have always enjoyed buying men gifts of an unusual and unique nature. I would always choose items that they would not normally have, things that would for ever hold romantic, glamorous connotations for them.

I agreed to any meetings he suggested because I wanted us to have as much time together as possible. On one occasion we met at a hotel in Grosvenor Square, just by the American Embassy, for dinner and an evening of intimacy, after which I had to go straight home to Sir Antony. The situation was already beginning to strike me as slightly ridiculous since the meetings always seemed to be rushed and rather furtive, hardly befitting a man of his status. In time, as he began to get to know me better, he started to unwind and tell me about his home life. I remember him telling me that he and his wife shared a huge bed so that they 'didn't have to have any contact with one another'. I was seriously bemused by this and couldn't image why they would want to keep up such a ridiculous charade. Sir Antony and I had had separate rooms almost from the beginning.

It was obviously very dangerous for us to continue meeting too often in hotels and restaurants and I decided we needed to have a place of our own. Hakim was selling one of his flats in Lyndhurst Court, which was quite near my home. 'If you are selling, Hakim,' I said, 'Sir Antony and I will buy it because we need a bigger place.' Since Sir Antony had moved into my beautiful apartment it had started to feel far too small. We both needed more space if we weren't to drive each other completely mad. I did not want to move immediately, however, and in the intervening months I used Hakim's flat to entertain Sir Peter. Obviously I knew that it would be terribly wrong and dangerous to take him where Sir Antony and I were living.

Although I enjoyed being able to pay for everything, and I wanted to protect his name whenever possible, I was beginning to lose respect for a man who would allow a woman to do this all the time and, in addition, would never bring the smallest token as a gift, not even when it was a special event. I was used to dealing with powerful men with high standards of behaviour and great courtesy and gallantry. Sir Peter never gave me anything except a small diary one Christmas, innumerable words of undying love and many, many letters. We talked a good deal whenever we were together and used to go for long walks with Coco and Pebbles in Regent's Park. As well as talking on a wide variety of other subjects, I was able to gradually turn to the subject of Sir Peter's future and how precisely we might be able to work together at some point further down the line.

I was surprised at just how difficult he found it to think expansively, considering his position, age and experience. Like Sir Antony, he didn't seem to have any real plans for what he would do once he had retired. I supposed that his energies had been so concentrated on his military career that he had not found the time to think how he could capitalize on his powerful position one he attained it. It occurred to me that when he retired he should set himself up as a consultant to the Sultan of Brunei. Brunei is an extremely wealthy state and is very pro-British, buying most of its military equipment from the British government, and I knew that the Sultan himself adored flying.

In my mind I had imagined that once Sir Peter had managed to get a foothold in Brunei, he would be able to get contracts from British companies eager to supply equipment such as Harrier Jump Jets and tanks as well as the undertaking of technical, military and strategic training. With my help and experience he could establish himself in just the same way as all the wealthy and influential middle men I had met in the Middle East and the USA. I spent a lot of time explaining to him just how the business world works and how fortunes can be accumulated just from having the right contacts in the right places. I could see he was interested, although he obviously wasn't exactly sure how to go about achieving it for himself.

I started my plan by making arrangements for a magnificent dinner for Sir Peter and the High Commissioner of Brunei, His Excellency Pengiran Haji Mustapha in the beautiful Oak Room at the Meridien Hotel in Piccadilly. There were to be ten of us at the dinner and to make the occasion more personal I insisted on bringing my own Lalique crystal, including a beautiful vase as a centrepiece for the table. I filled it with my favourite Casablanca lilies.

The High Commissioner's wife, Madame Norfishah Binte Sirirn, was enchanted with the place-cards which I had had written in calligraphy and slotted into my little Lalique card holders, which were all in the shapes of either doves, swans or pheasants. In my place, as the hostess, I had an eagle. Madame Norfishah liked the little crystal birds so much that afterwards I sent her the dove which had held her card, to thank her for coming. It is important to always thank everyone for their kindnesses. I am constantly surprised at how many people in high positions behave with such disdain and lack of courtesy when etiquette and good manners are in order. They seem not to know how to behave with originality, flair or good grace.

It was essential that there were enough people not to embarrass Sir Peter by making the objective of the evening too obvious, so as well as the High Commissioner and his wife, I also invited May Yamani and her husband Salahudin. May is the daughter of Sheikh Yamani, the former Oil Minister from Saudi Arabia, who was one of the most powerful and charismatic people in the world at the time of the international oil crisis. I had met May at a party given by her uncle Basil Fahidi, an extremely wealthy Iraqi friend of mine of long standing.

I knew that May's husband, Salahudin, a former pilot in the Pakistani air force, was in contact with the Ministry of Defence in Saudi Arabia and was keen to talk to Sir Peter about the agreement which had been made for the Saudis to purchase Tornadoes and other fighter aircraft from the British government in an operation known as Al Yamama, or 'The Dove of Peace'. Salahudin wanted to go into business with Sir Peter, which had been my own assumption from the very beginning. I invited Lady Harding to the dinner as well, but she didn't come, which was a relief as she would have been an embarrassment. I didn't tell Sir Antony about the dinner as I didn't think I could trust him to be discreet.

It proved very easy with my contacts and position as the wife of an MP to arrange the dinner. I simply called the High Commissioner with the invitation and told him who else would be there. I then rang his secretary to find out if there were any foods to which he was allergic or which he didn't like. I always prefer to chose what my guests are going to eat in advance, even if the setting is a restaurant or hotel, because I do not want them to have to interrupt their conversations to read menus and then have discussions with the waiters. So I always made a point of finding out beforehand everyone's preferences, although very few wives or secretaries have ever seemed to possess this information.

I arranged for the party to meet in the lounge area beside the Oak Room restaurant, where I had organized for the finest vintage Taitinger Rosé to be ready for them. I have always considered it important that dinner guests are given the opportunity to get acquainted before eating. We all sat down to talk for half an hour before going through to the restaurant. I don't necessarily believe in forcing guests to always sit between two people of the opposite sex. Some hostesses seem to do that without any thought as to whether or not the people thus seated will be of interest to their neighbours. It is much better to work out which individuals will have the most in common and the most to talk about, and put them together regardless. I have been to so many parties where everyone blindly follows the rules of etiquette without using their initiative or intelligence. Following the boring rules of society can be a guaranteed recipe for disaster; you must always put people together who are going to benefit from one another's companionship, achieve something together or prove mutually amusing.

That evening I sat Salahudin next to Sir Peter and they got on so well that afterwards Sir Peter asked me to organize another meeting for just the three of us. So I arranged for them both to come to lunch with me at the Connaught, a venue I know I can always trust not to allow in reporters or cameras. Salahudin and Sir Peter talked in more and more detail about the Al Yamama operation as well as other projects which were worth many hundreds of millions of pounds to Britain. Sir Peter did not pay me anything for these introductions and all the expenses of the entertaining fell to me. I felt the dinner at the Meridien to have been worthwhile as there was now an even stronger possibility that, once he had retired, Sir Peter and I could work together. My mistake was in thinking that he was experienced enough to visualize his role in the whole thing, my having made the necessary introductions but I did understand his clear refusal to do anything at all while still in office. The mistake he made was in taking for granted everything that I was doing.

Sir Antony and I continued to meet Sir Peter and his wife on social occasions, at which Lady Harding often used to complain that her husband had no money and that they were poorly paid. Finally, one day I said, 'Peter, please tell your wife not to talk to people like that. It is insulting to you, very embarrassing and extremely bad manners.'

'You are quite right,' he agreed, 'sometimes she forgets herself.'

During my time in Dallas I had befriended a man called Atef Mankarios, who worked for Caroline Hunt's hotel company, the Rosewood Corporation. Now, while I was seeing Sir Peter, I read that Atef had been made President of Rosewood and that they were managing the

Lanesborough Hotel in London. The Lanesborough was newly opened on the prestigious Hyde Park Corner site which had formerly been the home of St George's Hospital. It was a highly luxurious hotel, marketing itself as offering some of the finest and most expensive suites in London. I invited Sir Peter and Lady Harding to meet Atef there for dinner one evening, and Lady Harding's opening comment was, 'This place must be losing you a lot of money.' It was a completely inappropriate remark, but Atef took it in good spirit and ordered a bottle of magnificent vintage Krug for all of us.

Finally, after about eighteen months of biding my time with Sir Peter and having spent an inordinate amount of time, effort and money on trying to groom him to fit into my plans for the future, it became clear that, despite all the introductions, business contacts and work, he was not going to have the vision, ability, ambition or courage to press ahead with the various projects. That decided, I felt it was best to terminate the physical side of our relationship, which had never been particularly memorable anyway. I chose the Lanesborough as the venue for our final intimate encounter so that at least he would have the memory of a truly special night to cherish. I hired a suite for the night so that we could be alone together. The hotel provided me with my own butler and headed note paper for the duration of the stay and there was even a fax machine discreetly installed in one of the drawers of the desk. The beautifully panelled drawing-room overlooked Hyde Park Corner and the park beyond.

I arrived at about seven o'clock to make sure that the Beluga, smoked salmon and Dom Pérignon Rosé were all prepared and then arranged to pay for everything in advance. The hotel sent a chauffeur-driven car to pick me up from my home. I simply told Sir Antony that I was going out with a friend for dinner and that I would be back late. He was very jealous because he always wanted to accompany me everywhere, but I couldn't allow that because of his drinking and his indiscretion, so he was not particularly surprised that I said that I was going on my own.

I wanted to ensure that everything was perfect. I even ordered a little box of black chocolates in the shape of a woman's lips as I knew Sir Peter ate only dark chocolate. I also brought my own compact discs so that we could have romantic music for the evening. Dinner was served in the suite. He told me all the usual nonsense that men say at such times: how much he loved me and how much he wanted to be with me always. I find listening to men who talk constantly like this usually makes me want to laugh because I know only too well that they mean it either until their sexual appetites have been sated or they get back home to the security of their families, feeling pangs of guilt towards me when they leave and towards their wives when they arrive home.

'I wish that I could reciprocate all this generosity,' he told me as we made our way through to the luxurious bedroom, 'but I simply don't have this sort of money.' By then I knew the size of his income but chose not to say anything.

The evening over for me, I returned home at around eleven-thirty to Sir Antony while Sir Peter slept on in the beautiful suite, having told his wife that he was away on a business trip.

10

The Depths of Despair

I n December 1991, having been married for no more than a year, I finally asked Sir Antony to give me a divorce. I felt completely trapped by him, unable to have friends of my own, always having to keep everything I did a secret in case he reacted by shouting and raving at me. Unable to see any sort of future for us together, I felt very alone and at a complete loss as to what to do. He was in my home, drinking and smoking heavily and making the place filthy and untidy. If I asked him to try to change his ways he would accuse me of nagging him and being a bad wife. My freedom had been taken away from me and all my friends had now gone, frightened away by my husband's behaviour.

I did understand, however, that he must be feeling very insecure as he approached his retirement, although nothing I could do or say seemed to make him feel any better. I had always tried to provide for his needs but I now realized that this was beyond me and that the cost to me emotionally was proving too great. He had always told me that the reason he had divorced his first wife was because she had had affairs. I had been somewhat surprised at that because she was so unattractive, and now that I knew how insecure and jealous he was, I guessed he must have acted the same way towards her.

'I am a lost man,' he told me pitifully, 'I have nothing. I have lost my family and my work. All I have is you.'

I could see no advantage to either of us in prolonging the agony. I have always prided myself on being able to recognize when I have made a mistake and acting quickly and with expediency in trying to rectify it. I had no intention of living with this mistake; indeed, I intended to deal with it as soon and as painlessly as possible and I begged Sir Antony to help me. I went to a lawyer and petitioned for a divorce on the grounds of his irrational behaviour.

'Please,' my husband said in one of his calmer moments, having found out about my intentions, 'if you wish to divorce me, please wait until after the next general election. Then we can do it quietly.' Foolishly and against my better judgement, I agreed to wait in order to see him quietly through the election, at which he was no longer standing for Parliament.

Sir Antony was at home all the time because Parliament was in its summer recess, and he was drinking heavily, as was his norm, with my beloved Pebbles and Coco for company. Whenever I was out I was terrified that he might fall asleep with a lit cigarette or cigar in his hand and burn down the flat with himself and my poor little dogs trapped inside. In his boredom one day he searched through all my private things, forcing open a precious lacquered box where I kept Sir Peter's letters, along with a few other personal items.

Writing letters to me full of intimate details had always been a dangerous thing for Sir Peter to do, especially since he sent them to the flat where I was living with my husband. I once opened one of the letters in bed in the morning when Sir Antony was hanging around, and, realizing what it was, slid it down the side of the bed out of sight. Pebbles, who was a very tiny puppy at the time, gleefully picked it up and ran up and down the corridor with it, shaking his head from side to side as I tried to remain calm and retrieve it before my husband, seeing my anxiety, would guess that there was something awry.

Having found my private correspondence from Sir Peter, Sir Antony was now in possession of a trump card, and alternated between furious, spiteful jealousy and an almost evil glee at being in a position, should he so wish, to make use of the letters as a negotiating tool.

Just as I had feared and anticipated, once the general election was out of the way and Sir Antony was safely out of Parliament, he changed his mind about giving me my freedom. 'If you divorce me,' he announced, 'I will destroy you and I'll expose the airman now that I have nothing to lose.'

'Please, Tony,' I said, 'I beg you, whatever you do, give me a divorce.'

'I'm not going to.' He was adamant.

'Please, you can call me everything under the sun – say I am cruel, or a drunk, a criminal or unfaithful, but just grant me a divorce.'

'Well,' he scoffed, 'we'll see how I feel tomorrow.'

I had already spent a lot of money on my divorce solicitor, but it was only the beginning. Sir Antony began to play the cruellest of games, a sort of cat and mouse with my emotions. One day he would say, 'All right, you can have your precious divorce', and the next day he would change his mind and vow never to let me go. The solicitor advised me that I could have the marriage annulled on the grounds of non-consummation, but I didn't want to humiliate Tony like that, I wanted to help him keep his dignity. Eventually I told him that I would do just that if he didn't cooperate with me, but he just laughed.

'No one would believe you,' he said. 'It would be your word against mine and I have a daughter as evidence of my manhood.'

'Please, Tony,' I pleaded, 'if you give me a divorce I will give you a hundred thousand pounds.'

He eventually agreed to this arrangement but it was still to be a full two and a half years before I got my divorce on those terms and by that time I too was drinking heavily and coming close to killing him. For the whole period of time he was torturing me like this I was helping him financially and paying all the legal costs for both of us. I was exhausted but unable to sleep at night. We had been sleeping in separate bedrooms for quite a time by then, but after he had been drinking he would force his way into my room in the middle of the night, announcing optimistically that he was my husband that I owed him something as a result. I became very ill, crying all the time and on occasion fainting. I wasn't eating properly and it was like living with my mother and anorexia all over again. His behaviour in public became worse and worse. We would go out to lunches and he would announce across the table, 'My wife is having an affair with the Chief of Defence!' to anyone who would listen. Everyone seemed to be gossiping about me and there wasn't a single person who stood by my side.

In November 1992, as Sir Antony and I were still battling it out in our nightmare and travesty of a marriage, my friend Rosa had come over from Valencia to visit me. Going out in the evening was not a practice in which I indulged with any great enthusiasm any longer, but I was bored with staying in night after night and so I complied with Rosa's wishes. We went out to dinner to Mimmo d'Ischia, an Italian restaurant in Elizabeth Street, whose owner gave me a beautiful pink rose as we left. After dinner Rosa said she would like to go on to a club, so even though I felt like doing nothing other than going home to bed, I took her to the Dorchester Club in Park Lane which is a part of the Dorchester Hotel. Although not a member myself, it was known to me through the bar manager at the hotel, Giuliano Morandin. He had introduced me to the club manager, a lovely man called David Frentzel. The club had been open for only a couple of years and was established by the Sultan of Brunei, who owns the hotel, to rival Annabel's as the best nightclub in London.

As with the rest of the Dorchester Hotel, no expense had been spared in creating somewhere elegant and relaxed in which the affluent guests could relax. The main room was like a large drawing-room, with sofas, good carpets, fine paintings and a working fireplace. The discotheque was in another room and there was also an extremely good restaurant which could easily rival anything that even Paris could offer.

Rosa and I were sitting at a small round table in the bar at about eleven-thirty, drinking champagne, when a young man walked in. I probably noticed him, although I don't remember now. It was Rosa who pointed him out as he walked past. Her exact words, in Spanish, translate as: 'Look at that man in the jacket.' I remember that he was wearing black tie but, instead of sporting the traditional black dinner jacket, he had on a gold-brocade bolero jacket. Having walked past our table, he proceeded to the discotheque. He didn't stay there long, however, and came back to the bar area and sat at the bar sipping a glass of pink champagne. I was in conversation with Rosa at this point and no longer paying attention to the young man.

The next thing I knew, the head barman, a gently spoken and courteous Irishman called Liam, had come over and said that the man at the bar presented his compliments and asked whether we would care to join him in a glass of champagne. Although we were on the point of leaving, I asked who he was and was assured that he was a long-standing and reputable member of the club. Rosa and I then accepted the invitation and Liam conveyed our acceptance. The young man came over to our table after an extra chair had been drawn up. He introduced himself as Nicholas Sokolow and apologized for the presumption of intruding on our privacy. He told us that he had just popped in for a drink after attending a birthday party at Anton Mosimann's restaurant in West Halkin Street, having decided not to go home just yet. As we got chatting, he told us that he had an art investment management company which he was running with a partner in Jermyn Street. The partner was the man with the financial background and he was the art expert.

Apart from his being immaculately polite and well-spoken, one of the first things I noticed about him was that he had the most beautiful and delicate hands. He was stylishly dressed, spoke with eloquence, was effort-lessly elegant and had the most exquisite manners. It was as if he was from another age, a dandy in one sense, with a gentility that was almost feminine. He spoke languages, loved music and seemed quite at ease talking confidently on a wide range of subjects. Physically, he was of medium height, slightly built with receding dark-brown hair cut in a tradi-tional way. He was neither handsome nor particularly memorable, but there was something. Maybe it was the grace and ease with which he moved or the gentleness in his eyes, or his bearing, which was upright and unapologetic.

I found myself becoming fascinated by this man and wanted to find out more about him. He told us that he had been to university in Paris, studied art and learnt Italian in Florence before returning to England, where he had received a traditional English education. He then joined Christie's, the international auction house in St James's, as a porter. Over the next eight years he had worked his way up to become a director of the company, having spent a couple of years in New York, and after another stint in London he had left to go into business for himself.

He seemed very young, only thirty-one at the time, but was utterly charming. I seem to remember that we immediately embarked on a profound discussion about inner strength, insecurities and the effects of a difficult childhood. Rosa, whose English was good and who could follow most of what we were saying, was tactful and sensitive enough to realize that the two of us were rather taken by each other and left us alone while she went to the dance floor. We continued to talk and it began to dawn on me that here was a kindred spirit, a man who had also experienced adversity but who had not allowed it to overcome his kind, gentle and trusting spirit. I could tell that he was educated, came from a good family of mixed nationality and took pride in his appearance. From our talk that night it seemed that he was also sympathetic, honest and sincere. He asked me no personal questions except whether I was married, and I lied, telling him that I wasn't. Not in order to practise any deceit but because I felt my marriage was nearly over and in my eyes the relationship which I was suffering with Sir Antony could in no way be described as a marriage in the traditional sense. The name Lady Buck didn't seem to mean anything to Nicholas, which was a relief.

Suddenly it was two-thirty in the morning and Nicholas suggested that he drive us home, as he'd had little to drink, and then discreetly went and paid for all the drinks. His car, a monstrous old black Rolls-Royce of which he was inordinately fond but which reminded me of a hearse, was driven up and we embarked on the short journey to St John's Wood. We dropped Rosa on the way at a hotel in Marble Arch and as he helped her out she said to him, 'Please look after her.' My ability to lip-read has always been a rather useful asset. What I didn't know was ultimately how important his ability to look after me was going to prove.

We drove on, not talking much, and he dropped me outside my apartment block. He gave me his card. 'Would you consider it an imposition if I were to call you?' he asked politely. 'Although I would quite understand should you choose not to give me your number.'

'I would be delighted if you called,' I assured him, and in return I handed him one of my cards as well as the pink rose given to me earlier in Mimmo d'Ischia. Nicholas asked me where it had come from and when I told him he laughed and said that he knew the place well, as it was right opposite the house where he was born in Chester Square and was somewhere he had been going to, on and off, for twenty-five years. He saw me to the door and kissed my hand. He later told me that when he reached home he cut the rose short, placing it in a little silver vase, and put my visiting card next to it on his bedside table. Later, while preparing for bed and looking at himself in the bathroom mirror, he'd said out loud, 'That's her, that's the one for me.'

When I got to know Nicky better he confided to me exactly what had happened that made him offer Rosa and I that fateful glass of champagne. David Frentzel, the manager, who knew him well, had suggested to him that it would be appropriate to offer us a drink because he knew me personally. Nicky had been on the point of leaving and the suggestion had put him in something of quandary. Essentially he is a somewhat shy and reclusive person and the idea of offering a drink to two unknown ladies in a club was an experience both frightening and totally alien to him. However, he didn't want to upset David the manager and only hoped that either we would decline his offer or that it would be a brief drink. But it was one of those fateful evenings that could so easily never have taken place. Had Nicky not found the courage to send Liam over with the invitation, the next few years of our lives would have been very different; had he decided to turn left at the Hyatt Carlton in Cadogan Square and go straight home, rather than driving up to Park Lane, we would probably never have met and I might have missed out for ever on the wonderful feeling of falling in love for the first and only time in my life.

The next day he rang me three times and even went to the trouble of driving up to push a little *billet-doux* under my door. From then on he wrote to me every day and sent me the most beautiful flowers. Over the next few days we met again for lunch at the Inn on the Park and for tea at the Meridien, which was across the road from his office, and I was able to explain a little more about my situation. I'm not sure precisely when I fell in love with him, all I remember is feeling unlike I'd ever felt about a man before, really caring about him in every way and not being able to stop myself from doing so. I was terrified that he would be frightened off when I told him about Sir Antony. However, having done so, I felt an enormous relief, for it was quite apparent that he understood my situation completely and could see nothing that merited any forgiveness. Each time we met, he appeared with a little gift such as a copy of the poems of William Blake. Over the next few weeks Nicky became fully conversant with the extent of my predicament with Sir Antony, whom he could hear when we were on the phone together, for my husband would come storming into my room wanting to know to whom I was talking and shouting abuse at me.

I took Nicky to lunch at the Oak Room at the Meridien and invited Sir Peter Harding to join us. I knew that the Sultan of Brunei was very keen to set up a museum and I thought that Sir Peter should know Nicky so that he could have an art expert on call should the need arise. By then, Sir Peter and I had not been lovers for quite some time, but just friends and potential business colleagues. Ironically, the two men seemed to like each other instinctively. A few weeks later I persuaded Sir Peter to organize a dinner at his home for the Ambassador of Saudi Arabia, Dr Ghazi Algosaibi and some other friends of mine, including a senior executive at the Swiss Banking Corporation and his wife and a major-general in the British Army. Sir Peter, who, I think, was unaware of my feelings for Nicky, asked me to bring him along as my companion because he wanted him to meet his daughter (she should be so lucky). It was a delightful evening all told, although Nicky, as I knew he would be, was memorably unimpressed by Sir Peter's daughter. The following day the Saudi Ambassador sent us both signed copies of a book he had written on the Gulf War.

Exactly two weeks after we had met, Nicky took me for dinner to Mosimann's restaurant, where he was a member. He had arranged for a lovely corner table so that we could sit next to each other. Halfway through the evening, I asked Nicky what he really wanted to do with his life. He thought for a moment and then said without hesitation, 'Ideally I would like to take you to Paris and, on one of the bridges overlooking the River Seine, ask you to marry me.' For a man who was essentially very shy and reticent, this took a great deal of courage to say. I was so touched, and at the same time thrilled, that my breath was taken away.

Two days later I sent the most beautiful orchid plant to his office from my florists, Kenneth Turner, with a note saying, 'Yes my darling, I will marry you.' It was still some weeks before we were to make love for the first time.

Nicky was always very protective of me, offering continuous moral support as I struggled to get free of Sir Antony, whom I'd asked for a divorce two years earlier. One day Nicky noticed that I had a few bruises on my arms. 'Listen to me,' he said firmly. 'You have never struck me as the sort of woman who could do anything to merit being on the receiving end of this sort of behaviour. Do you not value yourself a little more than to casually accept the way in which this man is treating you?' And that was my turning-point. Somehow these words penetrated by resigned apathy and gave me the strength to do something positive about my situation. Nicky was quite right. I did not have to put up with such intolerable behaviour. Within days, I packed my husband's bags, threw him out of my flat and had all the locks changed. Sir Antony retaliated by talking to the Ross Benson column in the *Daily Express* and telling them that he was divorcing me on the basis of my adultery, although he did not go so far as to say with whom. Three days later, when I was expected Sir Antony for lunch so that we could have another go at discussing how we were going to sort things out, I received a call from a tabloid reporter.

'Bienvenida, I heard you and Sir Antony are divorcing. Could I come and talk to you?'

'What kind of article are you writing?' I wanted to know. 'Is it gossip?'

'No,' she assured me, 'it's a serious article for the women's pages.'

'Fine,' I agreed, eager for the opportunity to put across my side of the story. 'Meet me at my flat but be sure to come after two o'clock because I am having lunch with Sir Antony as we have things to discuss.'

Of course, she did not come at the agreed time, but arrived just as Sir Antony and I were sitting down to lunch, so as to catch us together. I had prepared grilled *crottins* of goat's cheese, with sesame seeds and truffle oil. I didn't have anything to offer her, so I gave her my lunch, treating her like a guest despite all the tension that was in the air between Sir Antony and I. There were also my two dogs to feed but all I had in the flat were some biscuits, and these had to suffice as I had not found the time to do any shopping. The journalist was very charming and I was very cooperative and open with her, but the next day the most appalling article imaginable appeared. It was so disgusting and spiteful I couldn't believe my eyes. It was a vicious attack, cheap and badly written and denigrating both of us. She said I was a 'nobody', an 'Essex girl' building my life on the back of British society. She said of Sir Antony that 'there was no fool like an old fool'. She even made fun of the fact that I had given my dogs 'Duchy of Cornwall' biscuits.

The rest of the tabloids responded immediately and set up camp outside my door with cameras, trying to find out who my lover was, so that they could keep running the story. I rang Sir Peter and warned him what was going on out of kindness and consideration to him. Although we had stopped our affair it was important that we were not seen together until the story had died down. After a few days during which I had to ask Nicky to stop sending me little notes, the media realized that they were getting nowhere and the photographers moved off to watch someone new.

All through these problems Nicky stuck by me, constantly giving me moral support, being kind and tender and helping me to cope with a very difficult time in my life. Once Sir Antony had left my flat, Nicky and I could meet more openly and we became even closer. We spent Christmas at my flat, which was the first time Nicky had ever been inside the front door. It was the most wonderful Christmas I had ever known because for the first time I was with a man whom I truly loved. It was all so relaxed and peaceful. I was madly excited by my feelings for him. Before I invited him into my home – not that there was anything wrong with his other than that it was not really to my personal taste – I had all the carpets changed and removed everything that had anything to do with Sir Antony. I didn't want any of the stains or mess that he'd left behind to remind me of the hell I had been through. I wanted to start afresh with the new man in my life.

Nicky and I were so swept up in our passion and love for each other, as well as the romance of being together for Christmas, that I decided I wanted to have his child and rashly did not give him the chance to take any precautions when we made love for the first time. It was irresponsible, reckless and stupid but we weren't thinking of the possible consequences as I was terrified of spoiling the beauty of the moment. For my Christmas present, he gave me the most beautiful Tiffany brooch in the shape of a spaniel with emerald eyes. I bought him a Cartier cigarette case in eighteen-carat gold which dated back to the 1950s and had a sapphire clasp. It was meant for carrying his business cards as I knew he didn't smoke cigarettes.

On Christmas Eve, when he arrived for the first time, I wore a beautiful couture gown by Katherine Walker in ivory silk, with pearls. We ate caviar and smoked salmon and drank champagne while listening to Tchaikovsky's First Piano Concerto and the soundtrack from the film *1492: The Conquest of Paradise*. The whole evening was utterly magical. That Christmas was the happiest time of my life to date. Love-making with Nicky was a totally new experience for me because I had no idea that anyone could be so giving, gentle and selfless. He seemed to know instinctively what gave me pleasure, what I wanted and when. He was the most sensual man I had ever met.

I must have conceived the baby over that first Christmas if not the first time we made love because by January I knew I was pregnant. I called Nicky at the office to tell him. The news came as a shock as he was not prepared for it and his response was less than enthusiastic. He was aware of the impossibly bad timing of my announcement, whereas I was rather thrilled. I was still married to Sir Antony and Nicky's financial situation had become temporarily precarious owing to problems with his company. Unknown to Nicky, there was also the added complication of Sir Peter and the media's eagerness to identify with whom I was supposed to have been unfaithful to Sir Antony. Nicky was too shocked by the news to immediately give me the love and support that I needed at that moment, although I think it only fair to say that he came around to the idea quite soon. He visited me at home that very evening, but I could see that he was not exactly elated about what had happened and was rather subdued and reticent. It was then that I decided not to discuss it any further and once he had left I decided to terminate the pregnancy. I made the arrangements without informing him because without his full support and endorsement

I didn't want to have the baby, even if it was by the man I loved.

I really ought to have given Nicky more time to get used to the idea, and I should have discussed it with him before taking the decision, but I panicked, afraid of losing yet more of my freedom if I didn't act quickly. A few days after the termination we were talking about what we would like to do the following Christmas, saying how wonderful it would be to spend our next festive season in Vienna. 'But, my darling,' said Nicky with pride, 'don't forget we will have a baby by then.' I bit my lip, not knowing how to tell him the truth.

Within a week of the termination I fell into a deep depression and tried to kill myself. Sir Antony was still refusing to divorce me and being abusive, I had aborted the baby of the man with whom I was so much in love and the whole of my future seemed so terribly bleak. I was married to a man who was intent on destroying my life, I had no family to speak of, was feeling ill and tired and the prospect of ending all the pain seemed so welcoming. I became very drunk, having started on vodka at ten-thirty in the morning and, after a light lunch with a friend at the Dorchester Hotel, I came home and took a massive overdose of sleeping pills and more alcohol.

Immediately after swallowing the pills, I remember thinking about how happy everyone would be if I did succeed in killing myself – apart from Nicky, that is – and I decided that I had no intention of giving them that satisfaction. I managed to ring Dr Rau and blurted out what I'd done.

'It's too late for me to do anything for you,' he said. 'Hang up the telephone and I'll call you an ambulance.'

I did as he had told me, gradually growing sleepier all the time. Then I somehow managed to call Nicky and told him about the pills, but I had to hang up because I was so drowsy and he was left not knowing where I was or where I would be taken. I vaguely remember the ambulance arriving within a few minutes and Jim, the very kind porter from downstairs, helping me out to the lift, but that is all. I was wearing nothing but a little silk slip with a mink coat over the top. I am told that Sir Antony, having been alerted to the emergency by Dr Rau, arrived just as the ambulance was taking me away and travelled with us to the Royal Free Hospital in Hampstead, but I remember nothing of the journey. At the hospital Sir Antony was given the mink coat, which had my house keys in the pocket. Nicky, meanwhile, was frantically ringing round every hospital in North London, trying to find out where I was. Eventually he tracked me down and turned up late that evening to find me in a public, open ward where people were crying out in pain, confusion and anguish. He explained to the nurse on duty that he was a very close friend and he was told that they had pumped out my stomach.

'You do know that she's pregnant, don't you?' he said to the nurse.

'Oh my God, no, she wasn't able to tell us that,' the nurse said, and came and asked me about it.

'No,' I told her, 'not any more.' The poor girl then left us to talk. Nicky was dreadfully shocked to see me in such a condition, on a drip, my make-up smeared all over my face, hardly able to speak or stay awake, and he was terribly concerned that I was so thirsty. He set about trying to make me comfortable, unable to concentrate for the time being on the news that I was no longer expecting the baby. He was terribly sweet and gentle and I fell asleep holding his hand. He later told me that it was one of the most harrowing experiences of his life. The following day Nicky brought me a pair of white track suit bottoms and a funny sweat shirt with 'Crazy Baby Mouse' written on it, and a pair of tennis socks so that I could walk out of the hospital. The nurses, who had been amazing, told us that my husband had taken my coat with the keys and my heart sank. Nicky drove me home with great care, stopping on the way at my local delicatessen to buy some provisions because I guessed that Sir Antony would be waiting at the flat, having been unable to resist the temptation to use the keys, and would probably require lunch. Nicky wanted to come up with me but I told him not to so he went off very reluctantly. Sir Antony and I had to sort it out between us.

As I had expected, when I got upstairs Sir Antony was still there, having stayed overnight, and he had opened my mail, including an invoice for the termination of the pregnancy. 'Oh well,' he ranted, oblivious to my condition, 'as if Sir Peter Harding were not enough, I have an even bigger story for the press now – pregnant behind your husband's back!'

'But you are not in my life any more,' I protested, 'so what does it matter to you?'

'I'm going to the papers,' he said, waving the invoice in the air, 'to show them this. This will destroy you and your airman.'

I started to prepare him a salad and smoked salmon, walking about in a daze, not really knowing what I was doing. He just kept going on and on at me until eventually I smashed the plates down on the table. 'For God's sake,' I screamed. 'I sometimes pray that I could get cancer because then

I could fight. You are worse than a disease, Tony, because I don't know what I'm fighting. Just get out of my life or I'll kill you!'

He left the flat then, but he didn't stop his attacks and abuse. Day after day he kept on at me down the phone, almost driving me to insanity. I drank and drank. Nicky was powerless to do anything but he stuck by me. However, I did feel a certain compassion, which Nicky understood, for Sir Antony, who had gone from being a distinguished public figure to a wretched, miserable and bitter old man. Therefore over the next two years I kept sending him money, clothes and food and let him look after my two dogs to give him some company and his loneliness, but still he kept phoning me with his drunken threats and insults, even going so far as to have a verbal go at Nicky on one occasion. Both Nicky and I continued to pay his bills until the end of 1994, even after he had remarried.

On 14 November 1993, exactly one year to the day after we met and three months after my divorce was complete, Nicky officially proposed to me at the Dorchester Club, where we had first met. It was a very special evening, although I did know that it was going to happen. As Nicky said, spontaneity is a wonderful thing as long as it is carefully planned in advance. I wore a stunning black Chanel dress with a PVC bodice and short skirt. The dress also had a unique accessory: a quilted PVC garter containing a little pochette. Nicky put my engagement ring in the garter before we left for the club.

The ring was an enlarged version of his signet ring, which he had ordered from his jeweller, Armour Winston of Burlington Arcade. It consisted of a beautiful Ceylon sapphire, a gemstone not mined since the last century, when the last mines were exhausted, and the jewellers had been obliged to hunt for an old stone before they could begin work on the engraving. The resulting ring is utterly beautiful.

After dinner Nicky took the ring from my garter and made the most beautiful, eloquent and moving speech, carefully explaining his decision to ask me to marry him and ending up by saying, 'We have already been through so much together and I have no doubt that we will go through a good deal more in the future, but I am in no doubt that you are the only person in the world whom I want to be beside me for the rest of my life.'

Nicky had never thought he would marry. Between them, his parents had been married six times and he was understandably cynical about the institution. His mother had told him many years before that she never wanted to meet any of his girlfriends and that it would be best if he eloped, and for this reason he did not introduce me to her for a long time. When I heard that she had gone into hospital for a minor operation one day, I asked Nicky to take her a note from me as an overture, and accompanied it with a little present: a beautifully dressed porcelain doll from Spain. His mother sent it back, saying that she was not in the habit of accepting gifts from people whom she had not met. I was very hurt and offended while Nicky was extremely embarrassed and humiliated. However, he continued to work at convincing her to meet me and eventually, shortly before we married, we did so. We became great friends for a while, even going shopping together, and I made sure I told her that I would always guarantee that she was number one in her son's life. She told me that I was her 'miracle girl' since she had never imagined that her son would find anybody who would be right for him. Nicky was thrilled and immensely relieved that the two women in his life for whom he cared so much were getting on well.

I had finally been divorced from Sir Antony in August 1993 and Nicky and I were married the following January. Originally we thought we would marry on 4 March, St Casimir's Day, because Nicky so wanted to have a son one day of that name. I remember that on New Year's Eve, Nicky and I were sitting at my glass table doing some paperwork. 'Oh, this is such a nuisance,' I blurted out. 'I'm having to fill in all these forms asking my name. Wouldn't it be simpler if we got married earlier?'

Without saying a word, Nicky calmly picked up the telephone, called Westminster Register Office and asked what was required to get married. Having duly made the appointment as suggested, we presented our various credentials, such as passports, birth certificates and my divorce papers, and were promptly married a week later, on 6 January 1994, by a charming lady in a green suit. It was my devoted housekeeper, Kathy, and her gentleman friend who kindly acted as our witnesses because at that stage we didn't have any friends we could trust. We didn't want anyone to know about the marriage in case Sir Antony found out and talked to the press again. I even took the slightly ridiculous step of wearing dark glasses on the way in and out of the building. We didn't yet want to tell Nicky's mother in case it endangered the fragile relationship we had just built up, although when we did so she was thrilled. That evening we went back to the Dorchester Club for dinner as husband and wife.

I was terribly happy to be married to Nicky, but I still felt that the rest of the world was against me. I was particularly concerned about Sir

Antony's persistent threats to go to the media with new stories about me and could see no reason why he would ever end his persecution of me, even if I gave him the £100,000 as agreed. I wanted to finish the business once and for all. I was confused and frightened and didn't know where to turn for professional advice. Then I saw a television programme about a publicist called Max Clifford. He seemed a reasonable and kindly man, skilled at helping show business personalities and other people who wanted to tell their stories in the tabloids. In my confusion, he seemed to me like the answer to all my prayers, someone to guide me through a jungle about which I knew nothing. I thought, if the papers were all going to write whatever they liked about me, as other journalists had done some time earlier, then I needed an experienced, professional adviser, someone to help me deal with the situation and put forward my side of the story regarding Sir Peter and Sir Antony. I thought that if everyone else is going to make money out of my misery, if they are going to treat me like this when I am a good, kind human being, then I might as well take the bull by the horns and make some money myself.

'I have an appointment to meet Max Clifford today,' I told Nicky over the cup of tea which he always brought me in bed, as he was preparing to leave for work a few days later.

'Who is Max Clifford?' he asked, looking over at me, never having read a tabloid newspaper in his life.

'A publicity agent,' I explained, and went on to tell him about my affair with Sir Peter, of which he knew absolutely nothing, and then what I intended to do about it. Strangely, he remained perfectly calm and listened to what I had to say without interrupting me.

'Get a good lawyer,' was all Nicky said.

11

Supping
with the Devil

*I*t is important to me that my side of the story is put forward before Sir Antony goes to the newspapers with his,' I told Max Clifford. 'Sooner or later the gossip is going to leak to the press and I would rather it came from me than from my ex-husband, who is extremely vindictive and therefore likely to distort the truth. Even the people who have been at dinner with Sir Antony and I and have witnessed his aggression towards me, even they are not speaking up in my defence. Sir Antony is threatening every day to go to the papers and reveal the details of my private life.'

I told him everything. I told him about my relationship with Sir Peter and about Sir Antony's intolerable behaviour, about the termination of my pregnancy and my subsequent suicide attempt. I asked him if there was any way in which he could assist me in dealing with the press, to help me put across the facts and stop Sir Antony from spreading any more rumours. He told me that he could do that, but warned me that the papers would need evidence of the affair with Sir Peter.

'I believe that there are security video recordings of all visitors coming and going from my apartment block and there may be one of Sir Peter coming to visit me. I think that the date was a few days after my birthday and I had invited him for dinner in order to break it to him in a gentle way that I had got married to Nicky. Surely that is evidence enough for the newspapers?'

I remembered that particular evening with great clarity because of Sir Peter's appalling behaviour. Not only was it a few days after my birthday, the date of which he knew perfectly well, but I also told him that I had married six weeks earlier and was blissfully happy with my new husband. Not only did he turn up empty-handed as usual but soon after dinner turned to me and made the unmistakable suggestion that we should become intimate together, saying, 'Shall we?' I replied that it would be best if he were to leave under the circumstances, which he did. After two years of this type of behaviour, I was fed up with his insensitivity, lack of consideration and persistent pleas of poverty.

'I think they will want a little more than that,' said Max. I had no idea at that time of the extent of the evidence that the papers would require.

I asked Max if he thought perhaps we should talk to a lawyer before we went ahead with the story, as Nicky had strongly suggested, but he persuaded me against this course of action, advising me that lawyers tended to gossip just like anybody else and that it would be best if I did not discuss the story with anyone. In any case, this would have broken any contract he might arrange with a newspaper. Strangely enough, he did introduce me to a lawyer of his choice but I was instructed not to discuss any aspects of the story at all with her. I never really understood the point of that particular exercise unless it was Max trying to cover his back. With the benefit of hindsight, I can see that I was not at that time in a fit state to make decisions or give interviews to journalists. I was ill and still drinking far too much. I just wanted someone to take care of everything and to advise me what to do. I knew that Max Clifford was a publicist who specialized in such situations and, trusting that he would be acting in my best interests, I was only too willing to place myself in his hands.

The reasons why I had sought Max's advice in the first place were that I had been grossly deceived and very badly presented in an interview which I had given the previous year. I had allowed a journalist into my home on the pretext that she was going to do a piece for the women's page and in fact what appeared was a rather nasty, vicious and misrepresentative article. Also, I wanted to go to the press before Sir Antony and finally, when Max told me that the story had financial value, I felt pleased because if I was to expose myself to the mercy of the press, doing it for free made no sense. After all, as far as I was concerned, this was a matter that had gone beyond the possibility of being settled quietly and amicably and as I had always considered myself a successful businesswoman, there was no reason to treat this any other way.

The newspaper which was ultimately chosen was the *News of the World*. A meeting was arranged with the deputy editor and at the same time I was introduced to Stuart White, who was to cover the story. Max explained the circumstances of my having approached him and told them that Sir Antony was threatening to expose me to the newspapers, that he had already told the *Daily Express* that I was an adulteress and that I wanted to be the one to break the story before my ex-husband could do any more damage. Both men were very charming and I felt very much at ease with them. However, they felt that in order to go ahead with the story they would need considerable proof that I was telling the truth.

Some time later I again met Stuart White, who said that I would need to arrange a meeting with Sir Peter, in order that we would be seen together, and record our conversation to verify the story. In this way their readers would be left in no doubt that he had acted with a terrible lack of discretion and had turned himself into a blatant terrorist target in order to be able to spend time with me. They believed that they had the story of a major security scandal in their hands but insisted that they would need very concrete evidence if they were to present the establishment with their revelations.

I showed them about twenty-five of the letters Sir Peter had sent to me: passionate, intimate letters full of declarations of love, in which he described my body and what he wanted to do to it, how much he worshipped me and how I was God's gift to men. Stuart wanted to see official samples of his handwriting to confirm that the letters were from him. I had in my correspondence file an official invitation from Sir Peter which conclusively corroborated this. I admired the professionalism which they brought to the job, but I felt uneasy about their pressing me to arrange a recording of a private conversation. It seems ironic to me that at this stage the press were so keen to verify all of my claims, whereas, when it came to some later revelations about me from unreliable and disreputable sources, they were prepared to print whatever they were told without a single shred of evidence. As to how much I ultimately received for my revelations and the subsequent newspaper articles, that will always remain a private matter between the *News of the World* and myself.

Once I had allowed myself to be persuaded to meet Sir Peter in a public place, I arranged for us to have lunch at the bar of the Dorchester

Hotel, a favourite lunching place of mine. It was agreed that Stuart White should be in the bar at the same time to witness how Sir Peter and I were together, so that he could write the story. It had been suggested that I should carry in my handbag a miniature tape-recorder in order to record the conversation. This plan was ultimately dropped by the newspaper's technicians, who were unable to guarantee that the machine wouldn't suddenly make an audible click. I had this vision of being in mid-conversation with Sir Peter and the machine suddenly making an involuntary noise which I would find myself at pains to explain. Instead it was decided to use a miniature microphone which would pick up the conversation and transmit it to a mobile listening unit parked close to the hotel. It later transpired that even this plan nearly failed to get off the ground as the van in which the technicians were recording our conversation had difficulty in finding a near enough parking space. So much for the best laid plans of mice and men.

Stuart White and the team wanted me to draw Sir Peter into a conversation in which he would not only confirm my story that we had formerly been lovers, but would additionally compromise himself by revealing military and security-sensitive information. This was quite easy as he normally did this anyway.

As planned, I met Sir Peter in the bar of the Dorchester and we had our normal lunch of smoked salmon washed down with champagne. The conversation was recorded and Stuart witnessed the entire event. After lunch we walked out of the hotel through the lobby just as we had done in the past and he kissed me goodbye before I climbed into my waiting taxi. The parting was recorded on video as part of the evidence and was broadcast, and stills were published, throughout the world. This single parting act, I now realize, was completely out of order and went well beyond the realms of acceptability. It appeared to everyone as having been callous, unnecessary and overly calculating, and it is something which I now regret. I genuinely feel that a mere photograph of us together would have been quite sufficient.

During the following week I spent a great deal of time with Stuart and the *News of the World* photographer in a variety of locations, including places where I had been with Sir Peter. I also worked on a thirty-second commercial to promote sales of the newspaper and this went out on television twenty-four hours before the story broke, in March 1993.

When I had first made up my mind to approach Max Clifford, Nicky and I had been married only a few weeks. We both knew that something had to change in order for the two of us to be able to enjoy our married life without being constantly worried about my ex-husband. Appropriately, I was the one who initiated proceedings by looking for a manner in which to rid ourselves of Sir Antony once and for all. Nicky was very supportive throughout this whole period but it was a severe imposition on his love for me. He did, however, find the manner in which I chose to expose the whole affair very shocking and was only able to take the whole thing on board because he loved me unconditionally. I did at one stage offer him the opportunity to walk away from the whole business and get back together when it had blown over but he chose to stick by me even though he found it all a great deal more difficult to accept than I did. We were perhaps naïve in underestimating the effect that my decision would have on our lives, which within a matter of weeks were turned completely upside down.

Nicky was appalled and in no way condoned what I was doing but stood by my side throughout, supporting me through what was an extremely fraught period, despite the fact that his values, priorities and ethics were being severely compromised. It showed a degree of flexibility and tolerance that I ought not to have expected from him but among the reasons why I had fallen in love with him in the first place were his calm dignity and endless patience.

Later we went to Nicole, my mother-in-law, for dinner. While Nicky was preparing dinner – he is an outstanding cook – I explained to her what was about to take place and she asked how much money I was going to make. When I told her she said that she would have been much happier giving me the money rather than my going to the newspapers. I explained that money was not the issue but that getting rid of my ex-husband was. I added that in the past I had never allowed anyone to manipulate me or my life in such a destructive manner and I was certainly not going to start now. As we were leaving after an excellent dinner, she held my hand tightly and told me that whatever happened she would stand by me.

Part of my contract with the *News of the World* was that I should be out of the country for a week, during which time they would break the story in two successive editions of the paper. My husband and I were given a choice of locations but selected Saint-Jean Cap Ferrat in the South of France. On the Friday before the first instalment we were flown out to Nice and then driven to the Hôtel Royal Riviera. It was and still is an extremely private and elegant hotel where we were treated with great courtesy and consideration. In all honesty neither of us was in a position to really relax and enjoy our week away. It was a tense and difficult time for us both because not only were we incommunicado with the outside world but we were aware that we would have to face the music on our return. Stuart White, who accompanied us, was still interviewing me, as the story was to be published in two instalments. All three of us became slightly paranoid, suspecting that any stranger was a rival newspaper reporter or clandestine photographer.

What happened after the first instalment was quite extraordinary. We did have access to satellite television and, of course, the British press, but we were unprepared for the bizarre and totally unfounded stories that began to circulate in the media. Apparently I was a spy, I was not Spanish, I was an impoverished aristocrat, I had supplied arms as well as information to Saddam Hussein during the Gulf War and finally I had been running an escort agency from a Mayfair address that was in fact my solicitor's. Incredible allegations appeared from anonymous sources and from family members with whom I had not been in contact for over twenty-two years. Even my mother behaved in an appalling way, telling totally fictitious stories to the press, and Paul, the man who had lived with her but had now been dead for a number of years, apparently found a way to give an exclusive interview from the grave.

Joining the ranks of this exclusive band was the father-in-law whom I had never even met. Nicky had broken off contact with his father some years earlier and when the story broke, my father-in-law gave an interview on the steps of his club in which he called me '. . . a scarlet woman . . .' and his thirty-two-year-old son '. . . a silly little boy who had never had a girlfriend . . .'. All this from the man who, I had heard, was a poisonous and dishonest individual and who, I later learnt, had allegedly been the father of an illegitimate girl by one of the numerous family nannies while still married and living with his wife.

There were others, however, who did display extraordinary loyalty and who behaved in a very honourable way. Kathy, my housekeeper, was totally devoted as well as discreet. The management staff of my apartment block also behaved with great dignity, the proof being that one of them apparently turned down a large cash offer from one or two reporters to allow them into my apartment in my absence. There were also well-wishers from Spain, America and England, all of whom knew me well and who believed that to take such drastic steps I must have been pushed to the very edge.

As a consequence of the newspaper revelations, Sir Peter resigned from his position as chief of Defence Staff. Only then did I have confirmation for certain that, despite his constant protestations of poverty, he was, in fact, on a salary of £110,000 per year, with a residence and staff thrown in. Also, it transpired that it was Sir Peter himself who had been behind a recent guideline for officers serving in Her Majesty's Forces in which a clearly defined code of conduct was outlined. Needless to say, this included the condemnation of extramarital affairs at all levels of the services. It is my understanding that after his resignation he went on 'holiday' and later returned to join the American company GEC as a director, his image apparently untarnished and still protected by the so-called 'establishment'.

A few weeks later I was invited, along with Max Clifford, to lunch at the Savoy Grill by the editor and deputy editor of the *News of the World*. I thought that the paper did its job very professionally even though I was not entirely comfortable with the manner in which some of the details were handled. As a result of the story, it went on to win the Newspaper of the Year award for 1994.

I can well understand that my revelations to the press and the consequent publicity did little to endear me to my new family. My mother-in-law changed her tune very quickly and chose not to have anything more to do with me. It was very honourable and brave of my husband to stand by me when his mother was trying to turn Nicky against me. Strangely enough, I remember an earlier meeting with Nicole in which she said that she wished that she had had a husband like mine. I do not blame her for her loyalty to her son but she ought to have understood that what I had done was so that I could find peace for myself and Nicky once and for all.

In June 1994 there was a further development. A previous acquaintance of my husband came forward with a story in which it was claimed that they had been having an ongoing affair during the early weeks of our marriage. It transpired that this was completely untrue but at the time I was unaware of this fact and, while I was in a furious, upset and drunk state, it was made clear to me that I could use this development to my advantage and gain yet further publicity. As a result of the allegations, I was badly advised by my then solicitor, as well as a few very misguided friends, who suggested that

I should organize a publicity stunt in which I would serve my husband with a divorce petition in full view of newspaper photographers. At the time I was in no condition to think or act in a rational way and I ought to have known my husband better than to believe such outrageous claims. If I had been thinking clearly, I would have sat down with Nicky and calmly discussed the whole business rather than listen to people who really ought to have been giving me better advice. I genuinely regret that little stunt, as well as acting on such bad and ill-judged legal counsel.

However, we should have known from our recent personal experience that nothing brings out people from the woodwork like a scandal and that this was no more than yet another attempt by a complete nobody to reap money from the press, who, at the time, were delighted to print anything in an attempt to discredit me. There was also a lesson to be learnt in that it is always the people who have nothing to lose who pose the biggest risks.

The incident was to bring Nicky and I even closer, as it now became clear that the most valuable, precious and trusty possession we had was each other. I now realize just how incredibly difficult things must have been for my lovely husband and how much support, loyalty, unconditional love and devotion he has always shown me.

It was a sad reflection on the low opinion that the press must have of couples who are in the process of splitting-up because, as soon as our intended divorce was reported in the papers, both my husband and I were offered substantial sums to reveal the intimate details of our married life. I even think that Nicky was offered more than I was. The nerve! Needless to say, all offers were turned down.

Despite being divorced from Sir Antony, I was still fighting in the courts to have overturned the order for me to pay my ex-husband the £100,000 which I had offered in order for him to divorce me. His threats to reveal my affair with Sir Peter were now no longer applicable and he had recently chosen to marry a Russian woman who had turned up one day on his doorstep after she had seen a photograph of him holding the two dogs in a newspaper in Russia. My husband and I were extremely generous over a considerable time to Sir Antony and Tamara, his new wife, despite their repeated drunken and insulting outbursts. Their ungrateful behaviour got to the point where we decided to call it a day and cease any further financial assistance. As a gesture of goodwill after our divorce, I had allowed Sir Antony to keep and look after Coco and Pebbles, my two King Charles spaniels, on the understanding that I was to have access to them whenever I wanted. Sadly, this was not to be the case. As for the order for the settlement of £100,000 this was eventually withdrawn and the whole lamentable episode of my marriage to Sir Antony officially closed.

12

Emerging from the Wreckage

*T*he initial media hysteria died down after a few weeks and this gave Nicky and I the opportunity to take stock of our lives. I was a great deal less traumatized by all the media hype than my husband, who found such an incredible invasion of privacy extremely difficult to handle. He had never before been the subject of such intense scrutiny other than at a professional level as an art historian and writer. As a result he found being dragged into the limelight on the pretext of something that did not really concern him undeniably hard to take in his stride.

There was still considerable interest in me after the furore of the revelations and this tended to be of a personal nature. Curiosity began to develop about the background behind my decision to go public and what kind of person I really was. The first person who seemed keen to get behind the image and find out what I was all about was Carol Sarler. She was interested in doing a feature for the *Sunday Times Magazine*. This I found rather encouraging as hers was a serious publication and she was offering me an opportunity to put forward the reality behind my background rather than have it distorted by media sensationalism.

Carol invited me to lunch at Claridge's, where I used to go with some frequency and which I knew would be a good and discreet environment in which to talk. I liked her at once. She was a very professional individual with keen insight who was also possessed of warmth and the ability to really get through to the person to whom she was talking. The lunch was most enjoyable, although at one stage I became rather emotional when Carol was obliged to go into the details of my childhood. Later she came to the apartment for the final interview. A photo-shoot was also arranged but this took place very late at night as I had to fly out to Madrid early the following morning and I was not very pleased with the photographs which were eventually published. They showed me looking somewhat stressed and rather tired.

Carol's article appeared in May 1994 and was very sympathetic, its opening paragraph reading: '. . . She's good, this lass, you've got to hand it to her . . . quite the gorgeous one, with a puff of hat and a sunburst smile. Porcelain bones, big eyes, little teeth, child woman. And it is in Claridge's dining room, an hour later, that she begins to cry. I had, clumsily, mentioned her childhood: unhappy days, unfit to probe. So I feel a wretch – is she really strong enough for this kind of interview? Later that night a friend chortles at my misgivings, my protective concern. "If she has this effect on you," he says, "just imagine what she must do to a man."'

Within a few short months Carol and I became friends and I was often invited to her lovely home. At times I would ask her opinion on certain matters regarding the media with which I found difficulty. Lowri Turner of the *Daily Mirror*, who also writes for women's magazines, was another journalist who showed me sympathy and understanding. She wrote in December 1995: '. . . I love clever, feisty women – bad girls who play high-stake games and win. I admire Lady Bienvenida for making all those men look like idiots.' Someone else who gave me a good deal of support and encouragement was Colin Wills of the *Sunday Mirror*. Luckily, as in any other line of work, there will always be journalists who are, in addition, good human beings and thus an asset to their profession.

I found that television was likewise an excellent platform for me. Even more so when it was a live broadcast because then nothing could be distorted or taken out of context. Television and press coverage of me and my life was not exclusive to England. There was enormous interest in me from France, South America and especially Spain, where I received a very warm reception on my first visit for a number of years, when I flew in with my husband in April 1994. On my return, Francisco Umbral, a leading writer and journalist wrote that I, Bienvenida, was Spain's revenge for the loss of Gibraltar. I loved that! There was a plan to name a street after me in Valencia, the city of my birth, and at one stage there was even a song about me which apparently proved very popular with Spanish youth, although I never actually heard it.

What pleased me most about my reception in Spain was that the media and television were more interested in me and my views on contemporary issues than in the scandal that represented such an insignificant proportion of my life. I lost count of the number of chat shows, game shows and debates in which I took part. The topics covered extended from politics and social issues to relationships and fashion.

There was one particular project which I undertook in Spain which proved most lucrative. This was a photo-shoot in which I appeared topless for *Interviú* magazine. The initial request was for a fully nude shoot but I did not feel altogether comfortable with the idea, so we settled on some elegant topless photographs in the presidential suite of the Palace Hotel in Madrid. It has always struck me as rather odd just how prudish women can be. Apparently they feel perfectly at ease sunbathing topless on a beach yet prefer their husbands not to see them in their underwear. This is certainly not the case with me. I have a good body at which I have worked very hard and I am not ashamed of it. If topless photographs were to have been published of me somewhere on a beach in the South of France, I would not have received a penny. Here was an opportunity to do virtually the same thing in a beautiful setting while earning a tidy sum, although it aroused my husband's strong disapproval. I remember his asking me whether, if he were able to raise the same sum of money that was being offered by the magazine. I would abandon the project. I simply replied that if that were the case, then we would have twice as much. The photos, which were accompanied by the story of my much earlier relationship with Thomas Enders, the former American Ambassador to Spain, were actually rather tasteful and ever since I have enjoyed a very good working relationship with *Interviú*. The account of my liaison with Thomas Enders was published in three successive issues of the magazine.

While I proved to be greatly popular in Spain, there was certainly no shortage of demand for appearances in England and Ireland. I continued to give interviews on a wide range of subjects, both for publication and on the radio, but television remained my best platform. On one occasion I was invited to Belfast to appear on Gerry Kelly's show. I was not familiar with either Mr Kelly or his show but was reassured that the show was highly acclaimed and that he was both charming and an excellent interviewer. However, it transpired that he had a little surprise in store for me.

As usual, I was warmly received in the studio and looked after with considerable respect. Nevertheless, this was not how I was treated during the course of the interview itself. I suspect that, being a man, Mr Kelly felt that by provoking me and trying to undermine my position he would prove himself popular with the audience. What he failed to realize, as have a number of other interviewers, was that the more I am provoked and my position challenged, the better I respond. As it turned out, the audience were rather shocked by Mr Kelly's attitude towards me and his totally unwarranted and unprovoked attack. After I had left the set, the studio was bombarded with supportive phone calls, in one of which a viewer said that if I had been a man I would have been perfectly entitled to punch the interviewer on the nose. It was also rather curious that Mr Kelly should have chosen me as a punch-bag, since the guest immediately after me was the former Irish Prime Minister, Albert Reynolds.

The other highlights, to date, of my television appearances have been *The Mrs Merton Show*, two appearances on the *Richard & Judy Show*, one on *GMTV* and my interview with Sir David Frost for *Through the Keyhole*. There have also been reviews of the British press for BBC radio and I was fortunate to have a number of articles published on fashion and seduction tips and pieces for St Valentine's day.

Perhaps the most challenging and rewarding project was the lecture which I was asked to deliver to the prestigious Oxford Union. I chose as a title 'Strategies for the Modern Woman', which would allow me to expound my views on a number of issues which I consider to be of importance to women trying to make a success of their lives in a male-dominated society. The address was delivered in such a way as to inspire women who had decided to take their future into their own hands and to become independent and powerful in their own right. This is in part because I myself have been able to fulfil most of my dreams through keeping everything that I wish to achieve in sight and working hard at every aspect of my professional and emotional development.

For a week before the lecture I was a gibbering wreck, unable to sleep and constantly badgering all my friends on everything from what I should wear to whether or not I should wear lipstick. As it happens, it was more the content of the lecture that concerned me than the prospect of addressing the assembled audience. I had represented Sir Antony on a number of occasions as the wife of a serving Member of Parliament, thus facing large groups of people and public speaking did not phase me in the slightest. And this time, once I had got the address under way, my nerves settled down. I was wonderfully supported by some admirers and a group of close friends, all of whom accompanied me to Oxford as if it were a state visit to the city. In my usual fashion, I took a suite at the Randolph and after the lecture hosted a dinner for my entourage and members of the union.

Addressing the Oxford Union, following in the footsteps of such great and powerful figures as Henry Kissinger, Caspar Weinberger, Mother Teresa, numerous British Prime Ministers and Kermit the Frog, was a great honour. My address was the result of my many years of dealing and working in the worlds of business and politics, both of which continue to be dominated by men. Despite the years of Margaret Thatcher's rule, I believe women are still regarded as weaker, less capable and more fragile than men and are continually coming up against the 'old boy network' when they try to succeed. Nothing significant has changed since the sixteenth century, when Michel de Montaigne wrote: 'women are not altogether in the wrong when they refuse the rules of life prescribed in the world, forsomuch as only men have established them without their consent.' There is a feeling among most men, and many women, that our gender should be confined to less serious activities than leadership and decision-making.

I believe that a modern woman is one who is prepared to struggle against the situation, confidently believing that she has the ability to succeed in any environment she chooses without compromising her integrity or allowing herself to be intimidated. A modern woman relishes her femininity and is aware that it is one of her most powerful weapons, and that her sensitivity, intuition and persuasive abilities should be used to her best advantage to fulfil her goals. Nothing undermines a man's posturing and aggression more effectively than charm, intelligence and grace.

A modern woman should be able to command respect through determination, ability and success. She should demand the highest standards in everything and refuse to allow men to make her feel uncomfortable in any of the traditionally male situations, such as boardrooms. A modern woman acknowledges as normal and in no way patronizing the traditional courtesies and good manners proffered by men in either a social or professional environment.

I feel that I can inspire other women because they can see that I came from a humble background and never allowed it to hinder my progress; and that I overcame all the negative aspects of my childhood with motivation, courage and ambition.

A woman's first strategy must be to take advantage of the many educational opportunities which surround us all, whether these lie within the formal settings of school and university, or are the informal opportunities of the outside world, and to learn from others of more experience. Success requires discipline and anyone with ambitions to get to the top ought to be aware that any mistakes made at an early stage will inevitably end up on the front pages of the tabloid press in years to come.

Despite my experiences among men of power – that they are inclined to fall from grace – I still believe strongly that the development of the world can be promising if it is placed in the hands of capable people. It is my view that at present we lack any great leaders because the people who rise to the top in politics are obliged to conform to such narrow-minded moral standards. Any man who has been unfortunate enough to make a mistake in his youth, perhaps had an affair or been involved with a business deal that did not work out, is then toppled through the media's apparently insatiable appetite for scandal and sordid revelations. As soon as anyone, man or woman, tries to stand for public office, they are regarded as justifiable targets for media intrusion and unnecessarily close scrutiny. Very few of the great politicians of the past would have been able to withstand the hypocritical and in-depth moral inspection to which our modern politicians are subjected. The legend of John Kennedy's Camelot would not have survived the scrutiny that Bill Clinton underwent while running for the presidency of the United States, where every affair he was alleged to have had was pored over in minute detail. Gladstone's interest in young prostitutes, whether philanthropic or not, would have made gruesome headlines, as would Lloyd George's mistresses, not to mention his habit of selling honours to the highest bidders. We need leaders who are larger than life, powerful and charismatic, which means that we must learn to be indulgent of their usually uninteresting little peccadilloes. Anyway, these rarely, if ever, have any bearing on their ability to make decisions about the future development of a nation and cannot be seriously regarded as undermining its stability.

It has never been more true than at the present time that the more successful we become the more envy we attract, but we must never allow this to make us timid or to deflect us from following our instincts. Nothing is worse than ending up regretting missed opportunities. The most important secret of success, I believe, is to never let your confidence slip, nor ever allow others to undermine it. We have to continue to hunger for success throughout our lives, thinking ahead, being patient and never sacrificing big, long-term gains for small, short-term profits.

I have now reached a stage where, for the first time in my life, I am blissfully happy. I am surrounded by warm, loving and trustworthy people who accept me for the person that I am. I have three new spaniels, Sasha, Moschino and Amaretto, who keep me fit, and as for feeling fulfilled, I am still full of ambition and kept constantly busy with numerous demands for television, radio and media interviews as well as quotes on wide-ranging topics. I am working on a variety of proposals from media networks and publishers and still find time to enjoy an active though select social life both in England and further afield. I won't deny that I continue to live in a very luxurious style but this is due entirely to my own endeavours extending over a long period of time. I have always valued myself very highly and ever since the age of nineteen have been accustomed to a high standard of living, of which I am justifiably very proud.

I do not apologize, nor am I ashamed of anything I have done. In fact, I am proud of my ability to have withstood the furore that resulted from some of the decisions I have made. But, with the benefit of hindsight, I feel that some of the aspects could have been better handled by the professionals whose help and advice I sought. There were also a few consequences of my decisions, some of which were rather out of my control, that did create some awkwardness and I of course regret having been the cause of some pain to those who least deserved it. Nonetheless I handled myself with considerable dignity and aplomb, given the pressure I was under, and am also proud of the fact that no one ever succeeded in getting the better of me or undermining my confidence and self-control at any stage. The problems with my ex-husband Sir Antony and the affair with Sir Peter represent a minute and rather insignificant proportion of my life and I have had no problem whatever in putting these behind me.

People in general have now discovered that there is a great deal more to me than previously reported in the press. I find nothing more gratifying than when, as happened very recently, complete strangers approach me when I am out shopping or walking my dogs and tell me how much they admire me and my courage in exposing the hypocrisy that is rife in society today.

I have not forgotten where I came from and, most importantly, just how far I have come. There is no ultimate goal, just continuing ambition, and I look forward with great anticipation to the challenges and undoubted excitements that are sure to present themselves in the years ahead.